I'D LIKE TO BELIEVE IN JESUS, BUT…

By Bob Siegel

I'd Like To Believe In Jesus, But…

Copyright © 2007 by Bob Siegel All Rights Reserved

ISBN-13: 978-1522824169
ISBN-10: 1522824162

Second Edition 2007
First Edition 1999

All Scripture quotations, unless otherwise indicated, are taken from NIV Study Bible, Red Letter Edition, Zondervan Bible Publishers, Grand Rapids Michigan.

No part of this publication may be reproduced, stored in a retrieval system, or transmitted in any way by any means—electronic, mechanical, photocopy, recording, or otherwise, without the prior permission of the publisher.

Printed in the United States of America.

DEDICATION

To my beloved children and children-in-law:
Elizabeth, Nathanael, Tori, and Lee.

PREFACE:
CHRISTIANITY - FALSE AND USELESS?

SIMILAR VIEWPOINTS IN DIFFERENT PLACES

I couldn't wait to see them. Bill and Carolyn were the parents of my best friend in high school, and they had always acted like second parents to me. Now, a college student, driving quickly to their home, I was anxious to arrive. I wanted them to be among the first to hear the exciting news: After years of living as a Jewish atheist, I, Bob Siegel, that loud – mouthed, self-centered, anti-religious character, had just met Jesus Christ through a dramatic and genuine mystical experience. Since my biological parents wouldn't be too overwhelmed by the news, perhaps my second parents, a strong church-going family, would react more positively.

They reacted all right, but in a manner that surprised me. For one thing, they were concerned about my enthusiasm. I was so wound up and excited, you'd think I was at, well, at a football game or something. But it can be dangerous to be this excited about religion.

"Calm down, Bob," they said in a gentle but firm manner. "Maybe you will want to talk to our minister. He can help you to take your new faith in stride as we have learned to do."

Now, let us take a quick leap forward through time. Ten years later, one of my students at the University of California at Santa Barbara came to me with some concern about our Christian club, Campus Ambassadors. (Yes, that's right. I never learned to calm down. Instead, I went into full – time campus ministry.) Her concern had to do with the emphasis that too many Christians placed upon evangelism.

"Why are we always talking about sharing our faith?" she asked with sincere bewilderment. "It seems to be emphasized a lot at our meetings."

She, like my second parents from years ago, had been raised in the Church. Christianity, to this young co-ed, was as American as apple pie, Chevrolet, baseball and the Waltons. But why did we need to share Christ with others, especially when they had religions of their own?

Since I entered into this whole thing through the back door, rather than a Christian upbringing, I found

her question somewhat ironic. As Christians, we supposedly believe that people are lost in their sins, so why would we not want to share the Gospel of forgiveness and deliverance? But I wasn't really caught off guard. I had long since learned that a lot of people in our country call themselves Christians simply because they were raised that way, not because they had ever given it much analytical thought. Many relate to their Christianity the way I once related to my Judaism. If you had met me in my B.C. days and asked my religion, I would have answered, "Jewish." If you had asked me what Jews believe, I would have said, "We believe in the Old Testament, but not the New Testament." But if you asked me a third question, "Do you personally believe in the Old Testament?" I would have said, "Me? Oh no. I'm not sure I even believe in any God at all." Yet I still considered myself to be of the Jewish religion, and the obvious contradiction of my answers would not have caused so much as a flinch. This paradoxical thinking, I discovered, was also characteristic of the way certain Christians interact with their faith.

Just as there are conservative and liberal synagogues (the latter explaining my shallow view of Judaism), so there are liberal Christian philosophies which "appreciate the traditions of Jesus, but wisely learn to dismiss such 'backwoods' ideas as *miracles* or belief in a *sin nature*." Is it any wonder that one can be in such a church and not understand evangelism?

But what about conservative churches (sometimes called Evangelical or Fundamentalist) that do believe in all of the biblical accounts? Many of them fall into a different trap. When asked by some skeptics how one can know that Jesus is truly the Son of God, they reply, "We know by faith." The answer is made to sound profound in its spiritual

6

simplicity. Those who ask questions in or out of the Church are viewed as being "too cerebral" or "too much into the head." "After all," they say smugly, "God works with the heart."

How surprised some of these Evangelicals would be to find out that their world view is remarkably similar to the unbeliever and the liberal Christian (both of whom they renounce).

Think about it. Why do most unbelievers take issue with Christianity? Why does the idea of Jesus being the only way to God or of Christianity being "the one correct religion" sound ludicrous and offensive? Because the underlying assumption, going into such dialogues, is that religion doesn't really have anything to do with the truth anyway. It's only a comfortable fantasy. Telling someone to choose Christianity over Hinduism or Islam is like arguing over *The Chronicles of Narnia* as opposed to *The Lord of the Rings*.

"They're both fantasies, so what difference does it make? Just pick the one you like."

Now, mind you, people generally aren't offended at the idea of a God. It's just the audacity of somebody explaining who this God is or claiming that God communicated which gets to them. Such assertions take God out of the fantasy category and challenge the notion that belief in God is a matter of faith alone. Question: If there is a God, would He not be integrated with reality? Could He not choose to make Himself known in as clear a manner as possible?

A PROBLEM WITH THE WORD FAITH

When they discuss other disciplines (history, science, math, politics), people are very interested in facts. But religion? That's a whole different story. This common approach may be understandable. Many religions do not offer facts. Even when we read the New Testament (which does offer them), we tend to look at passages about faith with a contemporary understanding. People mistakenly conclude that the Bible is asking us to fry our brains. They define a Christian as one who says, "I have no idea whether or not Jesus exists, but, hey, I know, I'll

7

just live my life as if He does and when I die, if it turns out that by chance I was right, God will reward me for having been so gullible and stupid." Faith is generally perceived as a blind leap in the dark; the naïve acceptance of an unsubstantiated teaching. Supposedly, God is fond of those who worship Him apart from any shred of data.

This popular description of faith is light years from the biblical definition. Actually, faith in Jesus' day was not defined the way twentieth century Americans use the word. In a paraphrased nutshell, the Bible says, "Since you know that God is real, it would be foolish not to place your faith in Him" (Romans 1:18-23; Acts 17:31).

New Testament writers verified the existence of God before ever mentioning faith. They were convinced that Jesus' resurrection from the dead was a fact (1 Corinthians 15). Most of them had witnessed it themselves and were confident that recent history would satisfy anyone who had not been there. Even more significant, the Holy Spirit continued to bear witness as He worked in the hearts of seeking people.

And this is how we know that He lives in us: We know it by the Spirit He gave us. – 1 John 3:24

In other words, a person could meet God! Faith, for the Biblical generation, had to do with trusting this God whom they'd just met to work in their lives.

Suppose I asked a friend to deposit a thousand-dollar check for me. It may take faith to believe that he will head for the bank instead of Las Vegas, but I will not doubt that my friend exists or question whether or not we really had a conversation.

This is the same kind of faith children have in their parents. One may count on a parent for food, shelter, love, attention, advice, etc., but children will have such dependence because they already know their parents. Likewise, since I am convinced of God's reality, I have faith enough to count on Him and obey Him.

My Christian pilgrimage has forced me to accept two depressing realities:

1) When it comes to religion, most people are not interested in truth. 2) Many American churchgoers are also uninterested in truth.

But Jesus said, *"I am the way, the truth and the life. No one comes to the Father but through me," – John 14:6*

These words must mean something and there is no law of literary criticism that can transpose them to read, "I am whatever you want truth to be. I am that zone of comfort which exists in your imagination to get you through your version of life." Maybe, instead, the words mean exactly what they say.

Maybe it's time to admit that if Christianity isn't true, it is meaningless. We should stop evangelizing. We should stop going to church. We should stop doing whatever we associate with Christianity.

And if Christ has not been raised, our preaching is useless and so is your faith. More than that, we are then found to be false witnesses about God, for we have testified about God that He raised Christ from the dead. – 1 Corinthians 15:14-15

9

INTRODUCTION:
DIFFERENT KINDS OF APOLOGETICS

AN APPROACH FOR HONEST SEEKERS

Although I hope Christians will enjoy this book and find it useful for those times when they are barraged with questions, the reader whom I primarily have in mind is the skeptic or doubter. The term *doubt* should never be viewed as a four – letter word. I have deep respect for those who ask questions rather than make decisions on impulse. Of course not all skeptics are members of the Humanist Club or scoffers of religion. Perhaps you were raised a Christian, but you've reached a point in life where you are now trying to decide for yourself what you truly believe. Or maybe you converted to Christianity hastily after some persuasive conference speaker gave an altar call or in the midst of a warm, friendly retreat. Possibly you are now slowing down, catching your breath and evaluating this decision. All skeptics are welcomed in these pages, both inside and outside the Church.

The purpose is simple: I am attempting to eliminate the barriers that might keep people from accepting the truth about Jesus Christ, His divine claims and His offer of salvation for the forgiveness of sin. The discipline employed is frequently called *Apologetic*s, a word commonly associated with certain second-century Christian leaders. Apologists differ from theologians. Whereas theologians seek to teach what the Bible says, apologists seek to defend what the Bible says to those who might not be convinced of its credibility. Early apologists verified Christianity in the face of Roman persecution, attempting to ward off certain accusations or misunderstandings and in doing so made the term *apologis*t a popular one.

Generally apologetics falls into two camps:

1) Academic Apologetics
2) Moral Apologetics

By *academic*, we mean questions such as the existence of God, the accuracy of the Bible or the historicity of the resurrection. Moral Apologetics, on the other hand, assumes (at least for the sake of the immediate conversation), that the Bible is in fact the inspired Word of God. It defends the commands and character of God in the face of those who would call Christianity an unethical religion. One very common question in this vein is the question of suffering: "If God is such a loving God, why is there suffering and evil in the world?" Here the skeptic is not asking for archaeology or fulfilled prophecy to authenticate the Bible. Instead, he/she is saying, "I have a hard time believing in a God who allows evil, and I would like to consider the Bible's explanation to see if it is in fact talking about a loving God. If it is not talking about a loving God, I will dismiss the Bible on moral grounds." Still, to even ask such questions, one must pretend for the moment that the Bible contains God's stated reasons. Sometimes the two disciplines slip into an overlap with each other, causing a very frustrating conversation. Observe the following example of dialogue:

Skeptic: (asking Moral Question) Why does a loving God create evil in the world?

Apologist: (giving Moral Answer) Well, actually God didn't create evil. Adam and Eve brought evil into the world by disobeying…

Skeptic: (interrupting with Academic Question) Now hold it right there. Evolution has proven that the Garden of Eden story is a myth.

Apologist: (now responding with Academic Answer) No. Many scientists don't believe in Evolution. Have you ever heard of Creation Research?

Skeptic: Yeah I have, and I think they're full of baloney.

See how the conversation so quickly drifted from one question to another? It began as a moral question and then turned into an academic discussion. The apologist would have done better to say, "For the sake of continuity, let us assume that the Bible is true since you are looking for the Bible's explanation. Afterwards, we can talk about the accuracy of the Bible or evolution or anything else you wish to discuss, but for now, you asked for an explanation of why evil came into the world. Do you see the explanation given in the Bible? Do you see how, if these events did happen, they describe a loving God?"

My purpose right now is not to get into a discourse on conversational skills but rather to illustrate how different the two kinds of apologetics are, and how seldom we stop to put them in their proper compartments. To help eliminate such confusion, the first part of my book will deal with Academic

Apologetics and Part Two will deal with Moral Apologetics. The latter section will be the longer one since those questions with emotional impact concern people more.

WHY THESE PARTICULAR QUESTIONS?

Many apologetics books have been written over the years. There are few that I have not liked. I hold a great respect and gratitude for both the scholars and the popular authors who have sought to answer criticisms of Christianity. As a matter of fact, so many such excellent books are available that I held off writing my own for quite some time. Often, after my talks, people ask whether or not I have written a book. Quite honestly, I wasn't sure that another apologetics book was needed. Then, as time went on, I noticed a very positive response toward the way I worded explanations including issues that Christians sometimes shy away from. For this reason, I decided to submit my own literary entry. But I was also extremely selective while choosing the subjects I wanted to include.

Each chapter (from Chapter 2, on) is a very specific answer to a painfully honest question—either a question seldom discussed or a question frequently answered, but with rhetoric many sincere skeptics have found to be simplistic and unsatisfying.

For example, although most apologetics books include a chapter defending the historicity of the resurrection, many of these books refer the reader to a logical process of induction regarding the various

13

theories of Jesus' missing body, yet this induction is based upon the assumption of certain historical events surrounding the trial and death of Jesus. When verifying these occurrences, the authors often quote extensively (if not exclusively) from the gospels. Although a case can certainly be made that the gospels are historically trustworthy, I am in complete sympathy with people who view this as circular reasoning. Therefore, much of my chapter on the resurrection (Chapter 2) will focus upon the testimony of Jesus outside the New Testament. Obviously that is not a new subject in the world of scholarship, but it may be new to certain readers unfamiliar with the ongoing debates. Likewise, I chose each additional topic because for one reason or another it seemed unique to me.

In Chapter 3, where we discuss the existence of God, I use the Moral Argument rather than the Argument by Design. Obviously I am not the first to use this philosophical approach, but I have found it to be a lesser discussed defense for theism. I also advance this argument to talk about the biblical God specifically.

In Chapter 4, where I seek to explain why God calls certain practices sinful, I challenge the readers to look into their own consciences to see if they actually agree with God, as opposed to automatically

embracing scriptures they do not yet believe in any way. Three difficult issues, pre-marital sex, homosexuality, and abortion are also discussed in this chapter.

In Chapter 5, I talk at length about a theology uncomfortable to Christians and non-Christians alike— Hell. In this discussion we will not only study what the Bible says about Hell, but we will also ask whether or not a loving, compassionate God could send people there.

In Chapter 6, we address another frequent charge against Christianity, namely its exclusiveness. Did Jesus really claim to be the only way to God, and if so, why did He make such a claim?

In Chapter 7, we get into a subject often brushed under the rug—"the people who never heard of Jesus." This question always comes up when Christians are trying to make the case that Jesus is the only path to God. But skeptics bring it up far more often than Christians address it.

Chapter 8 looks at the hardest question at all—God's commands to the ancient Hebrews to make war upon the nations of Canaan. Although few would argue with the theory of a just war, it is difficult to see why a loving God would command the genocide of an entire nation.

Certainly related to any discussion of Moral Apologetics is a response to a very harsh accusation given against the Bible, namely its "low, insulting view of women." In Chapter 9, I have presented this controversial subject for those readers who are inclined to dismiss Christianity for gender – related reasons.

The reader will immediately notice some popular apologetics topics that I have omitted. I say nothing substantial about prophecy, and very little about evolution or suffering. There is not much discussion about the credibility of the Bible either (however, that is woven in and out of Chapters 1–3). The absence of such topics in no way indicates their lack of importance. I encourage readers to acquaint themselves with books that already do a good, thorough job with those former issues.[1]

Throughout this volume, the reader will notice a kind of rhetorical argument between an imaginary skeptic and myself. All major questions and sub-questions are based upon real conversations I have had in my travels to different college campuses across the country. My hope is that the reader will relate to these questions. Indeed, you may find that I am putting your own thoughts into words on the page.

---

1 A suggested reading list will be provided at the end of the book.

PART ONE: ACADEMIC APOLOGETICS

Chapter 1
FOUNDATIONS

AN IMPORTANT STARTING POINT

Since this is a book about apologetics as opposed to theology, I will not spend a lot of time explaining the Gospel. Although it is certainly true that a misunderstanding of the Gospel is often a barrier even bigger than skepticism, I am going to assume for the sake of brevity that the reader is already reasonably familiar with the claims of Jesus.[1] Still, since I am defending the Gospel, some quick review is in order.

The Gospel message is actually a very simple one. *Gospel* means "good news", specifically the good news that God, at a certain point in history, became a man and walked the earth (John 14:8-10). This man (Jesus) was crucified for His teachings. Three days later, He rose from the dead, appearing to many eyewitnesses, proving that both His claims and standards were of God (1 Corinthians 15). But His death was not an accident. He died deliberately and, in some unexplainable fashion, paid for the sins of all people (1 Peter 2:24; 1 John 2:2).

His resurrection points toward the hope of an afterlife, a time when forgiven sinners can be bodily resurrected themselves and completely recreated or "born again" (Romans 6:5; John 1:12-13). These brand new people will live without sin in the presence of God and fellow repentant human beings for the rest of eternity (Romans 8; 1 Corinthians 15). As a promise or down payment of this future relationship with Christ, God's Spirit takes up residence within our own soul, proving His existence and helping us to live a better life by changing and eventually transforming our inward hearts and motives (Romans 8:1-17; Ephesians 1:13-14). The resulting relationship with God is something people must choose to enter into (John 3:36).

Certain questions in the chapters ahead will later on force us to take a closer look at some of the above theology, but for now, these are the primary beliefs of Christianity.

"That's a nice story, but I don't buy it quite so easily. Maybe the superstitious writers of the Bible assumed God's existence, but I don't. For all I know the resurrection of Jesus was a myth. As for the claim that Jesus was God in the form of a human being, how do we know that any God exists at all? And even if there were evidence for some kind of God, that wouldn't automatically prove the God of the Bible. Many other religions conceive of God in different ways."

Good, honest objection. And it brings us to the pivotal question: Is there or is there not solid evidence for the reality of God, specifically the biblical Creator? As I begin to answer with a definite affirmative, I must quickly add several cautions.

My first concern is that people frequently attach different meanings to words. Words like *proof* and *evidence* can be confusing, sometimes used interchangeably, sometimes not. For example, often Christians claim that there is proof for the existence of God and instead of proof, they offer evidence, perhaps some significant scientific phenomena of nature. What they offer may even be good evidence, but evidence is not the same as proof and eventually they get a smug rebuke: "Yeah, well, you still didn't actually prove anything."

Here are my working definitions of *evidence* and *proof.* I define *evidence* as "that which points to a high probability that a given claim is true." I define *proof* as "something establishing an absolute fact." I do not believe we can know anything for an absolute fact apart from personal experience.

If you were doing jury duty on a murder case, it is very unlikely that you would ever have genuine proof concerning the guilt or innocence of the accused. All you would have to go by is the evidence offered by those who claim to be eyewitnesses or perhaps the logic presented by an attorney as motive and probability were explored. Finally, based on everything you could see, hear, and think about the case, you would reach a decision. Your choice might very well stand upon good evidence and sound logic. There may even be a 99 percent probability that your decision is the right one. But let's face it; there will always be room for doubt. Why? Because you weren't there. You did not see the crime committed. Maybe there is a unique and mysterious side of the story that nobody has heard. Perhaps it is a clever frame-up. Who knows? Who really has full assurance? *Only a genuine eyewitness.* Her own senses would draw the final conclusion.

A scientist will tell you that nothing is proven unless it is repeatable. An honest historian would have to admit that without the use of a time machine, historical facts are really historical records pointing to a likely possibility. We have every reason in the world to believe that Julius Caesar ruled Rome. But is such documentation proof? After all, we weren't there. We trust the manuscripts; mere testimonies of human historians who we hope weren't lying or deceived.

If these illustrations seem blatantly simple, I submit to you that the most common objections to Christian evidence can be addressed in a similar manner. This seems hard to believe because people grant themselves the right to invent a whole new system of logic when religion has entered the conversation. Application of such "logic" to a more common situation would usually be unthinkable. Nevertheless, there are some understandable reasons why people approach religion differently. Before making my case, I want to identify three roadblocks. Each block is a bias compelling people to be less objective in their appraisal of Jesus.

BLOCK ONE: THE BIAS OF DESIRE

People have a tendency to believe what they want, and who wants to believe that they are condemned in their sin? A belief in Julius Caesar is harmless, for such a belief is not demanding upon our lifestyle. People may continue to live a selfish life whether Caesar ruled Rome or not. But they would think twice after gaining the awareness of a God who holds them accountable.

BLOCK TWO: THE BIAS OF NEGATIVE RELIGIOUS EXPERIENCE

Perhaps you have had a bad experience with church. Maybe as a kid you were dragged to Sunday school against your will. Maybe you used to throw spit wads as Mrs. Pumpernickel tried desperately to interest you in the missionary journeys of the Apostle Paul. You may have grown up listening to long sermons, anxiously looking at your watch to see how much of the game you were missing at home on TV as the pastor made his sixteenth point.

Or perhaps you were not raised as a Christian. Instead, you have merely encountered Christians. Maybe some obnoxious personality tried to shove the Gospel down your throat using all the tact of a lawnmower in a barbershop. Or possibly your rapport with Christianity had nothing to do with evangelism, but you have seen enough of life to observe that people who go to church often behave worse than the non – religious.

Hypocrisy is often cited as a reason to reject the claims of Christ and it is perhaps the most understandable reason. When the philosopher Bertrand Russell was asked why he never became a Christian, one of his chief complaints came from an observation that so few Christians seemed to take the teachings of Jesus seriously.[2]

A hypocrite is one who acts contrary to his/her words or beliefs. I do not think anyone (Christian or otherwise) is completely free of this trait. I must certainly confess to such re – occurring inconsistency. At the same time, I do not claim to be perfect because I call myself a Christian. My claim is that of a covenant relationship with God in which He is at work in my life, slowly but surely changing the inner character. I have many instances of downright rebellion against His rule in my heart. Even after I repent and focus on God as much as I can, all that means is that I'm better than I was yesterday but not as good as I will be tomorrow. What God does with me, He is willing to do with anyone. I am not superior or singled out in any way.

Although the "born again" person does not claim perfection, we must also keep in mind that many of the people who call themselves Christians are not really Christians at all. It is easy for people to use this title because of the strong Christian influence upon western civilization. This has created a variety of pseudo-Christian traditions, from the sincere, faithful church attendee who does not understand what it means to know Jesus personally, to the horrible bloodthirsty murderers of the Crusades and the Inquisition, who did not seem to share even the slightest resemblance to the simple, loving message of the New Testament. My own people, the Jews, have been hounded and murdered for centuries in the name of Christianity, and this shameful horror kept me blinded to the real Jesus for quite some time.

If hypocrisy is your concern, it may surprise you to learn that you actually have something in common with Jesus, for Jesus hated religious hypocrisy and preached against it quite often.

Not everyone who says to me "Lord, Lord," will enter the kingdom of Heaven, but only he who does the will of my Father who is in Heaven. Many will say to me on that day, "Lord, Lord, did we not prophesy in your name and in your name drive out demons and perform many miracles?" Then I will tell them plainly, "I never knew you. Away from me, you evildoers." – Matthew 7:21-23

This interesting discourse given early in Jesus' ministry proved to be very prophetic. Therefore, hypocrisy in the Church, while sad, is not a phenomenon which contradicts the words of Christ, for He not only spoke of hypocrisy, but hypocrisy in His own Name! Try to imagine some mere man, ambitious, anxious to start a following, gathering people together before things even get rolling and saying: "Can I have your attention? I just want you to know that many of you who call yourselves my followers will be cast into Hell by me personally. Just thought you should know." Not very likely. Such chilling honesty suggests from the onset that there is more to Jesus than meets the eye. He is making it clear that regardless of terminology or sworn allegiance, true Christians have two minimum qualities: 1) A personal relationship with God. The term *know* in Greek (prognosko) referred to an intimate knowledge, and 2) An obedience to God that follows this relationship. Although elsewhere in Scripture it is made clear that sinless perfection cannot be obtained in this life (1 John 1:8), Jesus is nevertheless emphasizing that true followers are at least on God's path and His words here in Matthew let us in on a little secret: Those who aren't truly on the road with God can perform mighty religious deeds—even supernatural ones. This is a scary and sobering thought. Still, we conclude that religious hypocrisy is not a genuine reason to reject the real Jesus and His true teachings.

BLOCK THREE: THE BIAS AGAINST MIRACLES

If the same number of eyewitnesses and historians who recorded the resurrection merely reported that a man named Jesus had started a revolution in 33 A.D., no one would doubt it. The incredible miracles associated with the resurrection understandably create tougher standards and greater skepticism. But are such special criteria fair, or do they instead close our minds to the witness of history? Think about it. If you are going to start by assuming that miracles are impossible, it will never matter to you how much evidence can be brought forth because all data will be immediately dismissed.

An open mind ought not to assume that miracles are impossible. After all, when the Bible talks of miracles, it is not assuming that God waved His hands like a magician and threw natural law out the window. God, as the author of life, is also the author of all scientific law. If science has taught us one lesson over the ages, it is that humankind frequently learns to do things previous generations would have thought impossible. Imagine somebody in 70 A.D. looking at a television set or a telephone or a computer. Imagine their expressions if they could watch a rocket blast off and land on the moon or if they could see a jet touchdown on a runway. To them, such technology would appear very miraculous indeed. Obviously to us, these are not miracles but rather a harnessing of scientific knowledge previous generations had not yet discovered. Likewise, it is easy to assume that human beings, one thousand years in the future (or even one hundred years in the future, when we see how fast recent technology has developed), will be able to do things which would absolutely baffle our minds. If it is so easy to believe that people will be able to do that someday, why is it so hard to imagine that God (if He exists) can do those things now? A true open mind will not assume that miracles are impossible because the testimony of science has actually provided evidence to the contrary. *Miracle* is just a descriptive word for something science currently cannot explain. Therefore, the resurrection or any other event in the

Bible should be examined with the same test we would use for any other historical event.

WRAPPING IT ALL UP

With this in mind, I can safely say that we have as much evidence to support Christianity as anything else in life accepted through "high probability." At the same time, a person can know Jesus through a personal experience as real as any other experience perceived through the senses. His Spirit can come upon you and make Himself so mightily known that you will actually be able to say, "I have met God." I know that sounds incredible, but that is the wonderful claim: *God can prove Himself to you!*

"But couldn't I be suspicious of this too? How will I know that I am not hallucinating?"

You know yourself. You will have to examine your heart honestly to see if you think you are being brainwashed. Keep in mind, however, that I am not referring to a mental state of faith, but an experience which identifies itself as a true encounter with Christ.

"Couldn't you just as easily ask me to suspend all judgment about green leprechauns until I actually meet a leprechaun? What about UFOs or unicorns? What about Santa Claus? People claim to have all kinds of unusual encounters. Why should I pursue Jesus and not the others?"

Because there is excellent historical and rational evidence for the existence of Jesus. This provides a better reason with which to seek Him out.

"So the evidence authenticates the experience, and the experience authenticates the evidence. Sounds like a vicious circle."

Perhaps. But that is as good as information can possibly be. *Let's face it: Our own personal experiences, along with the witness of other testimonies, are the only two criteria people use to establish facts.* Let me illustrate with a modern parable.

A college student named Kevin was approached in the Commons by his friend Roger. Roger had an excited and somewhat mischievous look in his eyes.

"What's up, buddy?" Kevin asked.

"Boy, have I got some good news for you," Roger said with a smile.

Roger proceeded to tell Kevin all about this cute sophomore named Carrie who had observed him from afar. Although Kevin could not recall actually meeting this Carrie, Roger insisted that she

existed and had seen Kevin at a few public gatherings such as rallies and football games. Since Roger was prone to play practical jokes from time to time, Kevin initially dismissed Roger's claim.

Later in the week, several other people, close friends as well as casual acquaintances, spoke to Kevin about the alleged Carrie. "Honestly, Kevin, she really wants to meet you but she's kind of shy. Still, she's a knockout and it would be worth your while."

Kevin was now finding evidence that Carrie existed, but he still wasn't sure because it certainly could be a collaborated hoax. He began to weigh the likelihood of truth versus fiction. Although he had no reason to trust Roger, some of the witnesses were people who did not have joking personalities. This, Kevin found significant. Others did not even know each other but knew Kevin. They too had spoken with Carrie. The abundance of witnesses seemed to increase the likelihood that Carrie was real. On the basis of evidence alone, Kevin concluded that there actually was a Carrie, but of course there remained a shred of doubt. After all, he never knew how far – reaching Roger's schemes might go.

How is Kevin ever to move from the likelihood of Carrie's existence to the conviction of Carrie's existence? Yes, the answer is simple: He must ask to actually meet her.

You can meet Jesus too. But perhaps your mind is so inclined to doubt His existence that you first need to examine some evidence. The evidence is abundant, but it will take you only so far. Eventually, you must invite Jesus Himself to communicate with you. This part is between you and God, but the evidence is something the following chapters will help you with.

If you still wish to doubt your experience with Jesus, I hope you will be consistent enough to doubt all of your experience. On the other hand, if the "absence of proof" leads you to doubt the evidence, I hope you will doubt everything else in science or history that is supported by evidence alone.

Some will claim we can always doubt our senses. Since we perceive everything through our minds, perhaps the brain is deceiving us. Maybe what we see, hear, touch, and smell is only imaginary. I personally find no need in discussing these possibilities. After all, nobody lives by such a philosophy. We can speculate about our senses, but all the while we are continually placing a trust in them. In fact, the moment someone challenges the credibility of Christianity, asking for factual data, I am quite safe in assuming that she will use her senses to examine the data.

APPROACHES WITH EVIDENCE

I am going to offer two types of evidence for the truthfulness of Christianity. The first will be historical. Although numerous events in the Bible have been authenticated, I will limit myself primarily to the resurrection. If evidence shows that Jesus rose from the dead, then we can assume everything Jesus claimed and everything Jesus taught is true, for only God has the power of life over death and obviously He would not resurrect a false, misleading teacher. Thus, the resurrection will not only demonstrate that Jesus is who He claimed to be, but it will verify that all of Jesus' teachings were correct, including His teaching about the Bible. Jesus believed in the Old Testament (Matthew 7:12), and He also gave special authority to His disciples who eventually wrote part of the New Testament (John 14:25-26; 20:22-23). The other New Testament writers are people who had a close association with the disciples. For example, Peter tells us that the writings of Paul are to be equated with Scripture (2 Peter 3:15-16). As you see, when starting from the historicity of the resurrection, we can then move in other directions to eventually authenticate the entire Bible.

But there is a different kind of evidence, the evidence of philosophy. Of course this fascinating discipline has many different schools. The Rational School (one of my favorites) simply asks the question: "What is the most likely possibility?" "What is logical?" "What makes sense?" Logic alone has its limitations, but logic is significant.

Chapter 2 will offer historical evidence for the resurrection. Chapter 3 will start over again from scratch and offer rational evidence for the existence of God. Then, it will seek to ask questions about what such a God would be like. This will return us to the Bible from an alternate route, demonstrating the logical likelihood that the God of the Bible is in fact the one true God.

SUMMARY

Personal biases keep us from exploring the claims of Christ with the same methods we would use to explore any other truth claim. When we put these biases aside, we discover both historical and rational evidence for the God of the Bible. Realizing that evidence can take us only so far, the reader will hopefully approach this God through prayer and ask Him to reveal Himself as He has promised to do.

---

1 For a detailed discussion of the Gospel message from this author, see *A Call to Radical Discipleship* (Mission to the Americas, Wheaton, Illinois, 1997) p.11-41.

2 See Bertrand Russell, *Why I Am Not a Christian.*

Chapter 2

IS THERE HISTORICAL EVIDENCE FOR THE RESURRECTION OF JESUS CHRIST?

AN INTERESTING CASE

If you have had any exposure at all to apologetics or even to popular Easter sermons delivered annually by Evangelical pastors, you may be familiar with a very common, very inductive defense for the resurrection of Jesus.

The case goes something like this: It is a fact of history that Jesus of Nazareth led a popular movement in ancient Palestine and was sentenced to death in 33 A.D. by the Roman Governor of Judea, Pontius Pilate. It is also a fact that Jesus was executed by crucifixion and buried in a sepulcher (a hollowed cave with a boulder blocking the entrance). Fearing that His disciples would steal the body and pretend Jesus rose from the dead, the Jewish religious leaders asked Pilate to put a Roman guard over the cave. Pilate complied. Nevertheless, three days later, the body was missing and over 500 people claimed that a resurrected Jesus had personally appeared to them. All this (according to the case) is historical fact. Now, with these facts in hand, the inductive reasoning begins:

Question: If the body was so buried and so guarded and still missing three days later—if these are the facts of history, what actually happened to the body?

"Did the disciples steal it?"

The disciples didn't even have the guts to stick up for Jesus while He was alive. Where would they get the courage to risk their necks by fighting off Roman soldiers for his dead body? One common rumor is that they did it at night while the Romans were sleeping. This is a story that the Jewish priests asked the soldiers to spread (Matthew

28:11-14, Justin Martyr, *Dialogue with Trypho the Jew*, CVIII). But it doesn't wash. If the soldiers were asleep, how did they know it was the disciples who came? If they were awake, why didn't they stop them? Remember, the Romans had conquered most of the known world. Certainly such a powerful nation had enough on the ball to guard one dead man's body. Also, we know from history that Roman soldiers on night watch slept in shifts so at least four soldiers had to have been awake.[1] We should rule out the disciples. They did not steal the body.

"Well, what about the Jewish Rulers? Did they steal it?"

These men wanted Jesus dead. They had captured Him, placed Him on trial, and convicted Him as a heretic before even delivering Him to Pilate. Let me say it again. *They wanted Him dead.* What possible motive could they have for taking His body and risking the rumor of a resurrection, thus jump-starting a revival amongst Jesus' followers? And even if they had the body (for some unimaginable reason), they could have used the body to their own advantage when the Christian movement began spreading like wildfire. They could have exterminated the fire with the greatest of ease: "He didn't rise from the dead. Here, we'll prove it. Look! His body! Come on. You can see it's Him. He was a popular figure. Everyone knew what He looked like. See? Jesus…dead!" That would have stopped Christianity before it even got out the gate. The only reason they didn't produce the body is that they didn't have it. Time to rule out the Jewish priests.

"How about the Romans guards? Maybe they stole the body."

The tomb was sealed by the Romans (Matthew 27:66). The Roman penalty for breaking into a grave and for breaking any seal was death.[2] Romans didn't give a hang about Jewish religion and no Roman soldier was about to risk his life for the body of a dead Jew. No, the soldiers didn't steal it.

A THEORY OF DESPERATION

One more possibility, commonly known as the Swoon Theory, has been suggested by many skeptics over the centuries and was made very

28

popular by a book in the sixties called *The Passover Plot*.[3] There are different versions of this theory, but it basically goes like this: "Jesus didn't really die. The drink offered to Him on the cross was actually a special drug that simulated death. You know, kind of like in the story of Romeo and Juliet. You see, Jesus wanted to stage some fulfillments of prophecy, so He perpetrated a terrific hoax. After the drug wore off, He snuck out of the cave, appeared to a few of His followers claiming to have risen from the dead and later died in some unknown, unfound location. Perfect plan. What a bunch of suckers."

True, it was possible for one to live for a very short while after crucifixion, but let's be blunt. He would not be in the best of shape. This was the most horrible and torturous form of execution the world knew in those days. Also, it was customary for Jews to wrap bodies in a cloth, almost like a mummy. Now catch this picture, for it takes a very creative imagination. The drug wears off. Jesus regains consciousness, slowly opens His eyes, gets up, and unwraps His own burial garment. Looking toward the entrance to the tomb, He sees the next challenge. He must now push the boulder aside with sub-human strength and single-handedly fight off at least four Roman guards. Face it. If He could have done all that, He might just as well have risen from the dead, for it would have been every bit as much of a miracle.

Anyway, that is my paraphrase of the common case. Actually it is a good case in many ways and I have great appreciation for the inductive process. However, the foundation here is the claim of historical accuracy for the facts surrounding Christ's death and burial. Frequently after talking about history, pastors go on to simply quote Scripture, leaving the skeptic little reason to believe that such "evidence" is really as historical as we were originally led to believe.

Fortunately, there is mention of these events in other documents which are contemporaries of the Bible, but before we look at them, let us talk about the Bible first because it too is a very accurate book historically and people assume the opposite far too easily.

THE HISTORICITY OF THE BIBLE

In my dialogues with university students, objections to the Bible are very common and very similar: "We can't use the Bible to defend the resurrection," they tell me. "That's too internal. You are using one book to verify itself. Besides, the disciples of Jesus were extremely biased. They loved Him. They believed in Him. We cannot trust them to give an objective report."

Part of our problem with the Bible in discussions like these is the preconceived image people have of the Bible. Frankly, Christians contribute much to this image. When people look at this special book, leather bound, with gold-plated pages and a personal name engraved on the cover, it seems like something so mystical, so spiritual and so subjective that it cannot possibly have anything to do with history or any other objective discipline for that matter. Our claim that it is the Word of God doesn't help much either. It may be a true claim, but the phrase "Word of God" evokes different meanings in different minds. Some take the description to mean that God practically dropped it out of Heaven wrapped in a white box with a blue ribbon. This of course is not what the New Testament writers claimed. Instead, they claimed to have written it themselves while inspired by God's Spirit (John 14:25-26, 2 Timothy 3:16). Whether or not one chooses to believe that the history surrounding Jesus was given with inspiration, the fact remains that it is *history* and must be studied as history.

We should also keep in mind that the Bible is not one book, but actually a collection of 66 different manuscripts penned by 40 different authors over a period of some 2000 years. Although several of the books were written in a poetical style, many of the books claim to be actual history and can be corroborated by other ancient documents and archaeology.

The New Testament itself (our primary focus if we are discussing the resurrection), is a collection of 27 different documents. Two of the four gospels were penned by actual disciples of Jesus—Matthew and John—and both of these men claimed to be eyewitnesses of the resurrection.

Notice John's words from a letter that he wrote subsequently to his Gospel:

> *That which was from the beginning, which we have heard, which we have seen with our eyes, which we have looked at and our hands have touched—this we proclaim concerning the Word of life. The life appeared, we have seen it and testify to it, and we proclaim to you the eternal life, which was with the Father and has appeared to us. We proclaim to you what we have seen and heard, so that you also may have fellowship with us. – 1 John 1:1-3*

Nothing in this wording even remotely suggests that John is inviting his readers to take a blind leap of faith. Instead, he talks as though the facts are out there for anyone who wants them verified. And he himself follows Jesus because of what he has personally witnessed, not because he was taught to follow Jesus in Sunday school.

Another Gospel writer, Mark, was a companion of Peter who penned Peter's version of Christ's ministry supplying us with a third eyewitness source. This was a common practice in those days: A man, not very literate, would employ the help of an assistant commonly called an *amanuensis*. Nevertheless, when we read Mark we are really reading the testimony of Peter.[4]

Were the disciples of Jesus biased? Of course they were. But are we to assume from this that their record is unreliable simply because they liked and believed the man they were writing about? I find such logic very questionable: "Show me an eyewitness or a historian who accepts the life and resurrection of Jesus as actual fact, but the men who knew Him, followed Him, lived with Him, listened to Him, studied with Him; none of them count." Really now. I doubt that such a standard would be placed upon any other figure of history.

The noted New Testament scholar F.F. Bruce, (Professor of Biblical Criticism and Exegesis at the University of Manchester, England), once discussed an interesting analogy to this whole subject of bias:

Nor would any historian ignore Sir Winston Churchill's *The Second World War* or Mr. Harold Wilson's 'personal record' of The Labor Government, 1964-1970 on the ground that the author occupied the position of Prime Minister during the periods covered respectively by these works and would therefore present biased accounts (F.F. Bruce, *Jesus and Christian Origins Outside the New Testament* William B. Eerdmans Publishing Company, Grand Rapids Michigan, 1977, p.15).

Think about it. Who honestly believes that Winston Churchill held a view of World War II free from personal bias? But the follow-up question is just as important: Would any historian in his right mind be uninterested in a book about World War II written by Winston Churchill?

Yes, the disciples were biased, but no more so than anyone else who writes history. In the case of Jesus, we also have records that demonstrate the biases of those who did not follow Him. This is an important point to note for now and return to later.

First, let us wind down our discussion of the New Testament attestation by taking a brief look at the author of the remaining Gospel, Luke. Although he was not an original disciple himself, he wrote as a historian and interviewed many eyewitnesses to the life of Christ. Observe his words:

> *Many have undertaken to draw up an account of the things that have been fulfilled among us just as they were handed down to us by those who from the first were eyewitnesses and servants of the word. Therefore, since I myself have carefully investigated everything from the beginning, it seemed good also to me to write an orderly account for you, oh most excellent Theophilus, so that you may know the certainty of the things you have been taught.*
> *-Luke 1:1-4*

Theophilus' identity is uncertain, but he seems to have been a Roman dignitary of some kind who sponsored an investigation into the matters at hand by a man reputed as being a factual historian. It is difficult for people to think of Luke as a historian, but only because they are used to thinking of him as a part of the Bible and the Bible (as mentioned above) is approached with the unfair image of being "just a religious document."

But Luke did write as an accurate historian. This has been verified by many scholars, including Sir William Ramsey, one of the most famous archaeologists who has ever lived. Educated in the German Tubingen School in the late 1900's where the Bible was torn apart according to popular (and extremely subjective) theories, Ramsey originally took it for granted that the Gospel of Luke was untrustworthy. This all changed when his journeys to the Grecian-Roman world and subsequent archaeological digs began to verify fact after fact as reported in the third Gospel and Acts (also penned by Luke).

One alleged Lucan error was his statement that Lystra and Derbe were in the region of Lycaonia and Iconium was not (Acts 14:1-21). This contradicts Roman writers like Cicero who said that Iconium was in Lycaonia. But in 1919, Ramsey found a monument that proved Iconium was a Phrygian city, not a Lyconian city.[5]

A more serious controversy involves Luke's date of the Roman census. This census conducted under the Syrian Governor Quirinius took place in 6 A.D. according to the ancient historian Josephus (Antiquities 18, I. I.). But Luke associates the census with the time of Christ's birth (Luke 2:1) which according to Matthew took place during the reign of Herod the Great (Matthew 2). We know Herod was dead after 4 A.D. We would seem then to have a fairly major contradiction. But in 1912, Ramsey discovered an inscription in Antioch stating that Quirinius had been governor twice. Although it is not mentioned where, this dual governorship could easily have been in Syria. Since we know he ruled as governor of Syria once, that is the likely location for his earlier term and the location Ramsey argued for.[6]

These are just two of the many ways Ramsey was continually impressed. He went on to write:

Luke is a historian of the first rank. Not merely are his statements of fact trustworthy, this author should be placed along with the greatest of historians (William, Ramsey, *The Bearing of Recent Discoveries on the Trustworthiness of The New Testament*, p. 222).

OTHER ANCIENT SOURCES

Many good books have been written on the accuracy of the Bible, and for that reason I will move on now and spend some time talking about the witness of Jesus outside of the New Testament, because that witness also is abundant.

We'll begin with the Jewish witness. Although the original church was made up primarily of Jews, most of the nation of Israel rejected Jesus as the promised Messiah, and the Jewish priests and teachers were particularly hostile to Him. In the Talmud (an ancient rabbinic storehouse of law, wisdom, and commentary), Jesus is described as both a sorcerer and an apostate.

On the eve of the Passover Yeshu was hanged. For forty days before the execution took place, a herald went forth and cried, 'He is going to be stoned because he has practiced sorcery and enticed Israel to Apostasy. Anyone who can say anything in his favor, let him come forward and plead on his behalf. But since nothing was brought forward in his favor, he was hanged on the eve of the Passover (*Sanhedrin* 43A, *Babylonian Talmud* from Tannaaitic period 70-200 A.D. Translation from Jacob Shachter, *Sanhedrin, Translated into English With Notes, Glossary And Indices*, Chapters 1-6 by Jacob Shachter, Chapters 7-11 by H. Freedman, London, 1948: Soncino, p. 281-2).[7]

Yeshu, of course, is the Hebrew word for *Jesus*. "Hanging" was another way of describing a crucifixion.[8] Apostates were people who broke from the faith and/or preached heresy. Jesus' divine claims certainly placed Him into this category. The idea of a mere man claiming to be the God of Israel was as outrageous and dangerous as false teaching could possibly be (unless, of course, Jesus was telling the truth). But the Sanhedrin (a Jewish puppet court, allowed by the Romans to have limited jurisdiction over internal affairs) did not believe His claim and had no recourse but to denounce Him as a traitor and blasphemer.

Now here's the big question: Why did the Talmud go on to conclude that Jesus was also a sorcerer? Because in those days, if you didn't like a religious personality but could not deny the fact that he was doing miracles, the only recourse was to call him a sorcerer or a tool of the devil. Although most Jews today will insist that they do not believe in Satan, Jews in Jesus' day certainly did. He was mentioned in the Holy Scriptures (Job 1,2) and he was viewed as a rebellious spirit who sought to deceive people by performing miracles as exemplified by the magicians of Pharaoh's court who imitated the miracles of Moses (Exodus 7, *Kiddushin* 49:b, *Babylonian Talmud*).

What we have then is a fantastic anti-Christian source with bias predisposed *against* Jesus, a source nevertheless affirming that a teacher named Jesus came to Palestine with incredible claims and an ability to perform miracles.

But the Talmud isn't the only extra biblical source. The Jewish historian Josephus (A.D. 37-100 approx.) talks briefly but matter-of-factly about Jesus. He did not live long after Jesus and could easily have encountered many eyewitnesses to the resurrection. He would also have had access to documentation unavailable to subsequent generations. We know Josephus was not a Christian. For one thing, he believed that the Roman Emperor Vespasian was the Messiah.[9] Also, a Christian would have spent much more time and detail documenting a movement which he felt was the most significant one in the world. Josephus' clear yet casual interest in Jesus indicates a desire to comprehensively list the influential men of his day, not a desire to spend a lot of time there as a biographer. In this manner, he mentions the resurrection almost off the cuff as though it wasn't even a matter of dispute.

Now there was about this time, Jesus, a wise man, if it be lawful to call him a man, for he was a doer of wonderful works, a teacher of such men as receive the truth with pleasure. He drew over to him both many of the Jews and many of the Gentiles. He was the Christ. And when Pilate, at the suggestion of the principal men amongst us, had condemned him to the cross, those that loved him at the first did not forsake him; for he appeared to them alive again at the third day; as the divine prophets had foretold these and ten thousand other wonderful things concerning him. And the tribe of Christians, so named from him are not extinct at this day (*Antiquities of the Jews* book 18 chapter 3, William Whiston translation, *The Complete Works of Josephus*, Kregal Publications, Grand Rapids Michigan, 1981, p. 379).

In all fairness to the reader, I must admit that this is a very contested and disputed passage. The argument goes like this: "Josephus could not possibly have written this paragraph about Jesus because he wasn't a Christian. Only Christians would call Him *Christ* and only Christians believe He rose from the dead."

Ironically, these same skeptics are usually the ones who begin their dialogue by saying, "Show me just one ancient historian, other than a Christian, who claims Jesus rose from the dead. If it were really so historical, people other than Christians would have known about it."

"O.K.", I respond, "Josephus, a credible ancient source whose writings are widely used by historians and archaeologists alike for their knowledge of the ancient world."

"Oh, well …yeah…but Josephus doesn't count. We know for a fact that the Jesus passage is corrupted, probably placed there by some Christian interpolator years after Josephus died."

"Oh, we know this for a fact, do we? Tell me, exactly how do we know it for a fact?"

"Because Josephus wasn't a Christian. Only a Christian would have claimed Christ rose from the dead."

"But you just asked me for a non-Christian historian."

This is called "having your cake and eating it too." Sometimes there is simply no pleasing people. You give them just exactly what they ask for and they dismiss it by engaging in circular reasoning.

The bottom line: *That passage exists.* It's there, in every extant manuscript of Josephus. The claim of Christian rewriting is an argument based upon silence and those are the most fleeting arguments of all. If one wants to make such a claim, the burden of proof is on him. This rebuttal is based upon three erroneous assumptions: 1) That Josephus could not call Jesus *the Christ* if he thought Emperor Vespasian was the Messiah, 2) That Josephus would have to be a follower of Jesus to believe He rose from the dead, and 3) That the phrase *"if it be lawful to call him a man,"* could not be used by anyone who didn't accept the deity of Christ. I will address these assumptions one at a time:

1) *Jesus* was actually a very common name in those days. Josephus himself mentions 14 different Jesuses. It makes sense to assume that by using the term *Christ*, [10] he is simply specifying which Jesus he is talking about instead of claiming to be a follower. We should remember that Josephus was writing primarily to a Greek and Roman audience. The term *Christ* would have had special meaning to a Jew, but not to the audience Josephus wrote for. To the Greeks and Romans, *Christ* would designate a certain revolutionary from Palestine, not a title.[11] This theory is supported by another text in which he actually says "Jesus, who was called Christ."

...so he assembled the Sanhedrin of the judges and brought before them the brother of Jesus who was called Christ, whose name was James and some others (or some of his companions) and when he had formed an accusation against them as breakers of the laws, he delivered them to be stoned (*Antiquities of the Jews*, book 20, chapter 9, Ibid, p. 423).

Interestingly enough, this passage (the only other time Josephus mentions Jesus Christ) is generally accepted by all scholars and probably reveals what Josephus intended in the book 18 passage—a mere identification, a distinction from other men of the same name.[12]

2) The idea of a *resurrection* was commonly taught by Jewish Pharisees, and Josephus tells us that he became a Pharisee in the very first chapter of his collected writings. Pharisees believed in a final resurrected Kingdom of God (*Sanhedrin* 90 A, *Babylonian Talmud*). This resurrection was discussed in their Holy Scripture (Daniel 12:2), and there was even a story in 2 Kings 4 describing Elisha (by the power of the Holy Spirit) raising a widow's son from the dead. Josephus accepted the Scriptures as the Word of God (*Against Apian* 609. William Whiston translation), and wrote himself about the prophet Elisha (*Antiquities of the Jews*, Book 9). Therefore, he could easily have accepted the resurrection of Christ on the basis of investigation, interviews with eyewitnesses, etc. He could comprehend the notion of a holy prophet rising from the dead without even flinching, without feeling obligated to number himself amongst the Christians.

3) I should point out that Jews believed in angels who could visit the earth manifested as human beings (Genesis 18), so this phrase "*if it be lawful to call Him a man*," in no way proves any personal belief on Josephus' part in the divinity of Jesus. However, in all likelihood, Josephus saw Jesus not as an angel but as a prophet and was merely trying to describe Him as an *unordinary* man by using an exaggerated figure of speech not uncommon to ancient Jewish writers.[13] Possibly the historian considered both possibilities, angel or prophet. Josephus, aware of Jesus' miracles, may have simply been playing it safe by saying, "I'm not really sure who Jesus was, but his impact is significant, and I remain open." Obviously when a word like *if* is used, no conclusion has been drawn. We can confidently add Josephus' testimony as a Jewish, non-Christian verification of the resurrection.[14]

But I have saved the best for last. Have you ever wondered where the disciples and Luke obtained their detailed information about Christ's trial, since they did not witness it personally? It seems that at least a good deal of it came from Pilate himself. It was standard of governors to make judicial reports and send them off to Rome, but Pilate went even further, writing a lengthy letter to Emperor Tiberius. In this letter, commonly referred to as *The Acts of Pilate*, he describes Christ's trial and talks candidly about the many events surrounding the resurrection, including all of the events discussed earlier about the guards and the tomb. He even goes on to describe other biblical accounts such as the stone being rolled back supernaturally, the darkness, the earthquake, etc. Finally, Pilate confesses his own conviction that Christ must have been who He claimed to be, a decision he unfortunately arrived at after Jesus' trial. Just think, events so compelling that the Roman governor himself re-evaluates the identity of Jesus. This makes *The Acts of Pilate* one of the most amazing and persuasive secular witnesses for the Gospel.

Now there is one problem and it's a significant one. This document doesn't actually exist today in any museum. That is, it doesn't exist anymore. It has either been destroyed in the passage of time or possibly lost and waiting to be rediscovered like the Rosetta Stone or the Dead Sea Scrolls.[15]

Before you throw down this book in anger at a writer who so quickly pulls the wind out of his own optimistic sails, let me reassure you that what does exist today are other ancient documents referring to *The Acts of Pilate*.[16] There are four such testimonies and we will look at them in a moment, but first it must be pointed out that much of the writing from the ancient world has been lost. Pilate's report is by no means a rare exception. It is not uncommon to reconstruct the likelihood of one source by looking at other sources.[17] As the noted scholar F.F. Bruce puts it:

> People frequently ask if any record has been preserved of the report which, it is presumed, Pontius Pilate, prefect of Judea, sent to Rome concerning the trial and execution of Jesus of Nazareth. The answer is none. But let it be added at once that no official record has been preserved of Judea which Pontius Pilate, or any other Roman governor of Judea, sent to Rome about anything. And only rarely has an official report from any governor of any Roman province survived. They may have sent in their reports regularly, but for the most part these reports were ephemeral documents, and in due course they disappeared (F.F. Bruce, Ibid, and p.19).

Justin Martyr, an early Christian apologist, made clear reference to a document called *The Acts of Pilate* in a letter addressed to the Roman Emperor Antoninus Pius in A.D. 150. Describing in detail the passion of Jesus he writes:

> And the expression "They pierced my hands and feet," was used in reference to the nails of the cross which were fixed in His hands and feet. And after He was crucified, they cast lots upon His vesture, and they that crucified Him parted it among them. And that these things did happen, you can ascertain from the 'Acts of Pontius Pilate' (*First Apology* 35:7-9, translation from Rev. Alexander Roberts D.D. and James Donaldson LL.D editors, *The Anti Nicene Fathers*, Vol 1, Wm B. Eerdmans Publishing Company, Grand Rapids, Michigan, p. 174-75).

Justin went on to list many of Jesus' miracles, such as the healing of the blind and the lepers. He also credits Jesus with raising people from the dead. This description of Jesus' deeds is concluded with the following words:

> And that He did those things, you can learn from the 'Acts of Pilate' (*First Apology* 48:3, Ibid. p. 179).

Justin assumed that this record still existed in the official Roman archives and that Antoninus Pius could verify the facts easily. Justin's whole purpose in writing his letter was to obtain mercy from the highest official in the known world, thus sparing the Christian community a persecution which was becoming so commonplace. It is unlikely that Justin would ask a Roman Emperor to check a document if he did not feel extremely confident that the document existed. Otherwise, he would be foolishly putting his own life and reputation at risk.

Another early Christian leader, Tertullian (160-220 A.D.) wrote to Roman officials about the unusual events surrounding the trial, death, and resurrection of Jesus. Discussing a time when the Roman Senate actually considered classifying Jesus as a Roman deity due to the miraculous nature of his life, he wrote:

To go back to the origin of such laws there was an old decree that no one should be consecrated a god by an emperor till he had been approved by the senate. Marcus Aemilus followed this procedure in the case of a false god, Alburnus. This reinforces my argument that among you, godhood is conferred by human approval; if a god does not satisfy man he does not become a god, so according to this it is for man to show favor to God. Tiberius then, in whose time the name of Christian came into the world, when a report of this doctrine reached him from Palestine where it originated, communicated to the senate making it clear to them that he favored the doctrine. The senate however, because they had not examined the doctrine for themselves, rejected it. But Tiberius stuck to his own view and threatened to execute any who accused the Christians (*Apology* 5, Alexander Roberts and James Donaldson *Anti-Nicene Fathers* Vol. 3, Hendrickon Publishers, Peabody, Massachusetts 1995, pp. 21-22).

In this same letter, Tertullian specifically mentions the armed guards at the tomb, the sealing of the sepulcher, the rolling back of the stone, the guards scattering, the earthquake, the darkness, the spreading of a false report about the disciples stealing the body and Christ's last words on the cross. After this long discourse he says,

All these things Pilate did to Christ and now in fact a Christian in his own convictions sent word of Him to the reigning Caesar who was at the time Tiberius (*Apology* 21, ibid. p. 35).

Eusebius (260-399 A.D.) also tells us that Pilate knew about Jesus' miracles and resurrection, and that he made a report of such matters to Emperor Tiberius (*The History of the Church*, Book 2, v. 2). A church historian commissioned by the first Christian Emperor Constantine, at a time when the pre – Christian Rome's documents were undoubtedly still available, Eusebius' witness is key.

Some will argue here that Eusebius was a biased Christian historian, but years earlier a non-Christian historian named Tacitus (A.D. 56-117 approx.) also verified Pilate's report. Writing about the great fire of Rome that Nero blamed on Christians and disliking Christians himself,

Tacitus sought to explain the origins of the movement.

> Their originator, Christ, had been executed in Tiberius' reign by the governor of Judea, Pontius Pilate. But in spite of this temporary setback, the deadly superstition had broken out afresh not only in Judea (where the mischief had started) but even in Rome. All degraded and shameful practices collect and flourish in the capital (*The Annals of Imperial Rome*, Chapter 14, The Burning of Rome, Michael Grant Translation, Penguin Books revised edition, 1989, first published 1956, p. 365).

A famous historian reputed in his own days as being extremely careful and factual, Tacitus would not have been prone to writing about a movement without first checking the Roman archives to see if he could not get the most accurate report possible.[18] As you can see, in talking about early Christianity, he referred to the trial under Pilate. We assume that this information came from Pilate's official report, for any other source would have been hearsay to Tacitus. He would have compared it to the definitive Roman record. Tacitus also suggests that something caused the Christian movement to break out afresh right there in Palestine after Christ's execution had seemingly died things down. I find this a very interesting description. If the death of Jesus had somehow discouraged and caged the Christian movement, what would it have taken to revive it? This is undoubtedly a reference to the many testimonies that Jesus had risen from the dead although obviously these were not testimonies Tacitus personally believed, given the way he is describing Christians elsewhere.

SUMMARY

Given the accuracy of the historical events surrounding the trial, death and burial of Jesus Christ, a good inductive process concludes that He rose from the dead.[19] This history is found in the varied and reputed witnesses whose writings make up part of the New Testament. Although obviously biased, such reports can be read alongside a quite different bias of the Jewish Talmud, painting a bad picture of Jesus but nevertheless confirming that He did miracles and was executed. The Jewish historian Josephus (not a Christian) supplies an even bigger piece to the puzzle and reports the resurrection as a historical fact. Finally, the report of Pilate himself provides many details about the burial and resurrection of Jesus. Although this document has been lost, four credible witnesses to this document still exist today, including the testimony of the reputed non-Christian Roman historian Tacitus.

Is there still room for doubt? Recall our earlier discussion about the difference between proof and evidence. All this is historical evidence, good evidence, but evidence alone. It can be doubted but no more than anything else in history that we have a tendency to accept. It passes any objective historian's test in terms of the many and varied sources and eyewitness accounts. Still, this is not proof. This is a "trail of bread crumbs" left by God for those who want to open their minds and seek Him in prayer. Then, as mentioned in my first chapter, one can actually meet this resurrected Jesus.

---

1 See Professor William Smith, *Dictionary of Greek and Roman Antiquities* pp. 250-51 for a description of a Roman guard. Also, the Roman writer Justinian in his *Digest* 49:16 mentions the penalty of death for Roman soldiers sleeping on their watch.

2 A stone slab found in Nazareth dating 50 A.D. states the death penalty for anyone breaking Roman seals or stealing dead bodies (*Volume Bible Dictionary*, Vol. 3., Inter-Varsity Press).

3 See Dr. Hugh J. Schonfield, *The Passover Plot* (Bernard Geis,1966). Ironically, Schonfield actually accepts much of the Gospels as historically accurate to support his theory, and presupposes that Jesus had noble motives for the "plot." However, he conveniently dismisses all references to a guarded tomb as historically inaccurate. This paves the way for his allegation that the disciples did in fact steal the drugged body of Jesus. Other writers throughout the ages have supplied different versions of the Swoon Theory.

4 See the writings of the church Fathers Iranaeus (end of second century, *Adversus Haereses III.* I.i in Eusebius H.E.V. 8), and Papias (130), (*Expositions of the Oracles of Our Lord*, in Eusebius H.E.III. 39).

5 *Joseph Free, Archaeology and Bible History*, (Zondervan Publishing House, Grand Rapids, Michigan, 1992) p. 271.

6 William, Ramsey, *The Bearing of Recent Discoveries on the Trustworthiness of the New Testament*, pp. 275 ff.

7 Jacob Neusner, who edited his own translation of the Babylonian Talmud, uses Schachter's translation for this passage and admits that the text "is omitted in censored editions of the Talmud and is not found in the standard printed text" (Jacob Neusner, *The Talmud of Babylon*,

An American Translation XXIII Tractate Sanhedrin, Brown Judaic Studies 84, 1984, Brown University, p. 74).

8 As far back as the time of Moses, it was a Jewish custom to hang executed criminals on a tree even if they had first been put to death some other way such as by stoning (Deuteronomy 21:22-23). Although the Romans crucified Jesus, handing Jesus over to Pilate for punishment was as close to executing the sentence themselves as the Sanhedrin could possibly come in those days. Even though crucifixion was not a Jewish form of execution, the Roman purpose in crucifixion closely paralleled the Jewish purpose in hanging. Jesus, in a manner of speaking, was hanged publicly for all to see. Setting such an "example" to other potential offenders was the Roman reason for crucifixion (Josephus, *War*, 7, Tacitus *Historia* 4, 3, 11). Therefore, the Romans as well as Jews shared the practice of a public example, even though they had different ways to execute people. Certainly Paul made the connection between the death of Jesus and the hanging described in Deuteronomy 21, for he actually quotes the verse in Galatians 3:13 while talking about Christ's crucifixion.

9 In Josephus' own writings (War iii 392-408) we see this belief. The Roman historians Tacitus (*History* v13) and Suetonius (*Vespasian* 4) also discuss Josephus and his view of Vespasian.

10 The terms *Messiah* and *Christ* mean the same thing, "anointed one." *Messiah* is derived from Hebrew and *Christ* from Greek.

11 The Roman historian Tacitus calls Christianity a superstition, but still refers to Jesus as *Christ* (*The Annals of Imperial Rome*, Chapter 14). Pliny the Younger, a governor who arrested Christians in 112 AD, also calls Him *Christ* (*Annals* 15:44, 2-5).

12 The quick reference to Jesus in Book 20 suggests that Josephus is assuming his readers are already familiar with Jesus, giving even more evidence for the existence of the previous writing.

13 For a fuller discussion of ancient Jewish writing style, see Chapter 7.

14 There is much more to be said about this disputed passage commonly known as the *Testimonium Flavianum*. So as not to get too tangential at this point, I will instead refer the reader to a special appendix on Josephus at the end of the book.

15 The Dead Sea Scrolls were accidentally discovered in a cave at Cumran by a shepherd boy in 1947. Some 40,000 fragments of religious documents were left there by the Essene community, a kind of Jewish cult existing at the time of Christ. These rigorous disciplinarians isolated themselves from the rest of Israel, choosing instead to live in the wilderness. The Dead Sea Scrolls provide valued information not only about the Essenes but the land of Palestine itself. Many portions of the Old Testament were also found amongst these scrolls including the complete book of Isaiah, dating approximately 150 B.C. Prior to this discovery, the oldest complete Old Testament text, (the Ben Asher text) was dated at about 1010 A.D. When the Ben Asher text is compared with Isaiah, we see very little difference. Therefore, the Dead Sea Scrolls bridged a gap of over 1,000 years, demonstrating that the Jewish scribes who copied the scriptures, did so with great care and accuracy. As you see, scholars had to wait a long time for this terrific attestation of the Bible. Undoubtedly other such discoveries will be made as archeological digs continue in Israel.

The Rosetta Stone was discovered in 1799 near Rosetta, a city in Northern Egypt. An inscription written in Greek as well as Egyptian hieroglyphics, it provided one of the first clues toward the interpretation of hieroglyphics.

16 There is an Apocryphal *Acts of Pilate* also known as *The Gospel of Nicodemus*. This forged document, created sometime after the fourth century, is not the same Acts which I am referring to, although its author undoubtedly wanted it to pass as such.

17 For example, the teachings of Socrates come to us primarily through the writings of Plato.

18 A letter has survived from Pliny the Younger, a Roman Governor over the province of Bythinia in which he writes to Tacitus, "Thank you for asking me to send you a description of my uncle's death so that you can leave an accurate account of it for posterity....I know that immortal fame awaits him if his death is recorded by you..." (*Epistles* 6:16). This says something about the reputation Tacitus had amongst Roman citizens. And obviously, the very preservation of Tacitus' works also says something about his reputation.

19 For a fuller treatment of this inductive process see Frank Morison, *Who Moved the Stone?* (Zondervan Publishing House, Grand Rapids Michigan).

Chapter 3

IS THERE RATIONAL EVIDENCE FOR EXISTENCE OF THE BIBLICAL GOD?

PREMISE

On college campuses, I frequently attract attention to my outdoor open forums by putting up a large challenging sign that says in big bold letters: "Atheism Is Inconsistent."

The sign is not intended as an insult. It is instead, an attempted return to the rich heritage of universities in which different philosophies were constantly tested and debated. Debates can be done civilly, with respect, although I must admit that these days the appearance of such a sign looks unusual and provocative. Still, it does bring people around. Before long, I am confronted by that first brave soul, usually some confident-looking intellectual who is just ready to teach me a thing or two. "Why is atheism inconsistent?" he asks.

"Because nobody lives as an atheist," I say. "If we cannot live according to our own philosophy, the philosophy becomes questionable."

"I live consistently as an atheist," he answers. "I don't believe in God. I don't attend church. The Bible has nothing to do with my life."

"I believe you. I believe you sincerely think that God doesn't exist. I believe you live your life seldom, if ever, thinking about God. But if God did not exist, certain other truths would follow. Neither you nor anyone else live consistently with the *implications* of His nonexistence."

"What do you mean by that?"

THE IMPLICATIONS OF GOD'S NONEXISTENCE

There are only three possibilities that account for our universe. Any theory, scientific or philosophical, would have to fall under one of these broad categories.

A. It came about by accident, apart from a creator.
B. It always existed, apart from a creator.
C. It has a creator or creators. (It is easy to assume with our bias that Creation was the work of a monotheistic God. To enter this discussion with an open mind, we must admit the initial possibility of several creators. For the sake of easier communication, however, we will refer to the idea of "creator or creators" with the familiar word, "God" and the familiar gender, "He".)

Theories A and B would indicate that life is meaningless. Our intuitive and universal belief that life should have meaning had to come from somewhere. Even those who aren't searching for a general purpose to life often think about personal value. The very idea of such value had to have a source. Therefore, we can conclude that value and meaning came from a source outside of ourselves.
Theories A and B do not account for such possibilities. For this reason, we are left with Theory C: "Some kind of God exists."

DEFENSE FOR THE PREMISE

People claim to live without a sense of God, but the real truth of the matter is that no one lives as if he/she were here by accident.

When asking a skeptical science student how our beautiful and complicated world came about by mere chance, I was exposed to an interesting answer: "Look, it took billions and billions of years. It only makes sense that things would finally come out right."

"What do you mean by 'right'?" I said. "If life is an accident, there is no such thing as right and there is no such thing as wrong. If life is an accident, what is—just is. All opinions about right and wrong would be just that, opinions."

Do you consider yourself to have personal worth? Do you attach importance to your life? Would you expect from others the same respect, appreciation, love, and acceptance that they would expect from you? Do you feel a need to discover personal gifts and talents so as to make a valid contribution of some sort? Would you be bored and discontent doing unfulfilled work? Would you be satisfied with mere survival apart from happiness? Is happiness possible apart from what was just mentioned? If not, then we stand in full agreement. Without personal value, life is chaotic.

At the same time, if humans don't have a universal purpose, there is really no such thing as genuine value. Value becomes a mere invention, a hopeless dream. All that we work for, fight for, and stand for is ultimately unimportant. Even if we can't find this purpose behind life, the acceptance of a mystery is preferable to disbelief. Without such meaning, individual pursuit turns into vanity. We very much like to feel that someday, somehow, our experience will count for something. But without God, such an idea is nonsense. Why? Because *there can never be a purpose behind accidental creatures*. Just think: Success, freedom, human rights, none of these "virtues" have any coherence apart from the notion that we are genuinely precious.

"Well maybe life is an accident. Maybe we simply create value to enjoy ourselves more."

Why does one need to create value to enjoy himself more? If we really don't have value, where did such a preposterous idea originate?

"Maybe our thoughts of value were also an accident. Not everybody agrees as to what is important and what isn't."

Certainly variations exist, but we agree on more than the average person takes time to notice. The ultimate certainty for human worth is frequently ignored, yet obvious as your own thumbnail. I am referring to the conscience, that inward reflection appraising all thoughts, all motives and all actions. With unexplained intuition, people sense a responsibility to live with ethics. This is a firm contradiction to the theory of chance existence. If my neighbor is a mere accident, I owe my neighbor nothing. I am without moral obligation. After all, where would a mere fluke obtain the right to pass judgment? There could be no standard with which to measure his/her idea. Let us, for a moment, examine the obvious. Why would we consider it despicable to lie, cheat, steal or murder? Why does one feel bothered over a selfish, inconsiderate decision? In fact, why should it be inhumane to walk out on the street and shoot the first person we see?

"Oh come on. Of course it would be immoral to kill. What right do I have to shoot another human being?"

A good question. What right *do* you have? But finish your question. What right does the victim have to not be shot? Does this challenge sound horrifying? Only because the worldwide condemnation of murder is outrageously clear. Now think for a moment and try to analyze the situation. What really makes an action good or bad?

Once, while sparring with an atheist, I said to him, "If I were to conduct an experiment and steal your pencil, I could actually defend my move on the basis of logic alone. In fact, it would be impossible to condemn the theft by way of a proven standard. You will, of course, tell me how wrong it is to take what belongs to another. But such declarations flow from mere assumption. Could I not question your starting point? Why is it wrong?"

"It's wrong because stealing is against the law," he replied.

"But people willingly chose to establish those laws. Remember, moral presuppositions existed before the law was invented. As another person here by accident, no better and no worse than anyone else, I challenge those presuppositions. No, the law will not do. I will need a better reason if you want your pencil returned."

"Law or not, everyone knows that it's terrible to steal."

"How do we know? The argument of 'everybody says so' can lead to frustrated, circular reasoning."

"But these people are bearing witness to an obvious truth: 'Stealing is wicked and corrupt.'"

"All you are saying is that stealing is evil because stealing is evil. Again, this is not an answer."

"Here's a reason: We should respect our fellow man."

"Why should we respect our fellow man?" "Because people have rights."

"On what authority do we assume that people have rights?"

Do you see my point? We could go on for days and never get anywhere. Some of life's most basic facts are really subjective, unexplained feelings. This does not mean that the feeling is imaginary or mistaken. Not at all. We don't ignore our sixth sense simply because it can't be analyzed. It suffices to say that our knowledge of ethics is unaccompanied by reason.

To live consistently as an atheist, one must admit that all morals are invented. One must deny the validity of a universal moral standard residing in every conscience. In short, one must become a Moral Relativist. But Moral Relativism is quicksand. Nobody *can* live that way consistently. Sometimes a philosophy sounds clever in the classroom, but as soon as a student walks out the door of this classroom and finds that his bicycle has just been swiped, he no longer feels so sophisticated about the origin of ethics.

I usually meet moral relativists in the context of religious discussions. Sooner or later in our conversation, they express concern about religious hypocrisy. I always ask, "Are you morally outraged by religious hypocrisy?" When they answer "Yes," I say, "How can that be if there is really no such thing as morals?"

Forgive me for using more graphic and horrible examples: If someone broke into your house and murdered one of your loved ones right before your eyes, would you say to yourself, "Well, as one accident to another, I guess I can't be dogmatic here. In my opinion, what this person did was wrong, but since that is only an opinion, who am I to judge?" I don't think you would react that way. But such would be the *consistent reaction* of a Moral Relativist.

The last time you read in the papers that a woman was raped, did you think deep inside, "Clearly that rapist had a different set of values than me. Oh well." I know. This would sound like a joke if it weren't such a disturbing illustration. Of course, you didn't react that way at all. You cried out with indignation. You said, "This evil person must be brought to justice!"

There is no logical explanation for the conscience. An action is wrong simply because it is wrong. That's all we know. Further information has never been needed to persuade us of the right decision. Looking only at ourselves, we come face to face with a most baffling mystery. This is where a creator moves easily into the picture. Perhaps our joint, intuitive sense of judgment and accountability finds origin in a Being who will literally hold us accountable. It would be difficult not to at least consider this possibility. The illogic of morality as an end in itself takes on a whole new light when we consider a probable source. We are now drawn back to a closer examination of the creation/accident question.

The conscience will immediately condemn any individual who fails to treat his fellow man with love and respect. This awareness of "due respect" supports the certainty of human value. We already established that value could not be authentic apart from a universal purpose. Simple as it sounds, we have stumbled upon a path for the searching soul. *One can easily move from morality to value to purpose to a God who established this purpose.*

"Hold on. This is sliding by just a little bit too fast. Let's back up a minute. The conscience seems to be your focal point. I can concede the likelihood of God if there were no other explanation for morality. But many people pose plausible ideas for the birth of standards."

The general humanistic explanation is commonly called "The Wolf Pack Theory." The theory goes something like this: A long time ago, society learned that in order to survive, it would be mutually beneficial for people to treat one another with consideration. Laws were introduced in the event that some individuals did not wish to reciprocate. *In other words, mere convenience is mistakenly called "morality."* It's not that I sense any inherent value in humans. It's just that I treat you well in the hopes that you will do the same to me. The conscience is a habitual system of thoughts, derived from "the wolf pack."

This theory can be easily tested. First of all, those who appeal to the explanation frequently do so in the name of relativism for the purpose of excusing some alleged sins. "Since morality isn't real," they say, "I'm entitled to develop my own rules. You therefore have no right to judge my actions." But if it is wrong for me to judge, then there is such a thing as *wrong*. With the same breath in which morality is questioned, morality is confirmed.

Another problem with "The Wolf Pack Theory" is that frequently people do convenient things at other people's expense. They still feel guilty. Where did the guilt come from if self-interest and convenience are supposedly the whole reason we even have standards to begin with? It's easy to talk about cavemen and the origin of laws, but the truth is, I have only the experiences of my own life with which to decide what is right or wrong.

Supposing you were undercharged ten dollars by the cashier at a grocery store. You know that it will not be discovered until the end of the day when they total the register. You will not be caught. You can get away with this. What is the convenient thing to do? The convenient thing is to keep the money, of course. But would this decision make you feel guilty? If so, how do you explain your guilt?

"Brainwashing could explain the guilt. It may be that people feel bad for simply acting contrary to the very way they were brought up. The origin of this standard is something they never questioned."

53

People who ask for evidence of a God usually consider themselves to be free thinkers, and I agree with them. This sudden, about-face insinuation that they are actually brainwashed is most interesting. After all, once we realize we were brainwashed, we are not brainwashed anymore. Therefore, we should be able now to dismiss the voice of our conscience and sleep well at night. Try to imagine yourself keeping that money from the grocery store without guilt. The guilt should not be there. Supposedly, you were just brainwashed into believing that it is wrong to rip people off and you have now risen above such a delusion.

"Some people *do* commit crimes without any feelings of remorse."

Yes, and there is a name for such people. We call them *psychopaths*, implying that there is something terribly wrong with their minds. A psychopath is one with a warped or broken conscience. Calling something broken is not the same as implying that it doesn't really exist. The very label *psychopath* demonstrates that people really do see the conscience as something genuine, but malfunctioning in a particular case. Likewise, some are born without an ability to walk, but we don't take that to mean that legs are only imaginary.

"But many who have a working conscience still live immoral lives."

That is the greatest argument that we didn't invent our moral standards. If we were going to invent something, wouldn't we invent something we could live up to better? Ever since the traceable beginnings of history, the world has known war, crime, greed, hatred and bloodshed. Our technology has improved, but our nature is as barbaric as ever.

For a while, it was popular to believe that our species was evolving into a more civilized, compassionate being. The Nazi holocaust completely obliterated this fantasy. It made Nero's Rome look like a picnic by comparison, and yet it happened in the twentieth century. People representing every range of career, personality, age, and social class performed deeds that stunned the world. The world should not have been shocked. When the pressure is turned on, man's true nature erupts to the surface like deadly molten lava. People experience a wickedness which they never thought possible. Those who live in a peaceful environment can easily submerge this evil side, but the evil remains.

Even in everyday life we see people making selfish, callous decisions all the time, while the conscience tells us not to behave that way. This suggests that the conscience is coming from some entity outside of ourselves.

"Isn't it true that different societies produce different morals?"

Yes. But almost every single culture at least agrees that people should be treated with respect.[1] This is the one moral which is universal. For example, in some Middle Eastern countries, it is considered polite for dinner guests to burp after a meal while still sitting at the table. In America, that would be considered impolite. What's interesting is that both cultures agree that people should be polite.

"What about racist organizations or those older societies which corporately enslaved others? Here, we do not see even the standard of respect."

They aren't obeying the standard, but the standard to respect people still exists. What we see is a redefinition of the term *person* or at least the term *good person*. When slavery or any other human evil is justified, some kind of rationalization occurs. Hitler succeeded in recasting the Jews as villains before persecuting them. He assumed that such propaganda was necessary. He did not assume that he could just kill Jews for no reason and have nothing to answer for. African Americans were labeled as sub-human by many in the Pre-Civil War South.[2] Why? Because for wealthy slave owners to admit that all people were the same would be to admit that slavery was evil. Humans are notorious for figuring out ways to disobey their consciences.

It is true, however, that certain types of brainwashing do occur when rationalization is taught. Mark Twain illustrated this truth in

Huckleberry Finn. Young Huck, because of his background, felt guilty for helping his slave friend Jim escape down the Mississippi because he had always been taught that to assist a runaway slave was wrong. At the same time, Huck knew that he would feel guilty for refusing to help poor Jim. What was confusing for a young boy need not be a mystery to us. We see the brainwashing of a cruel slave-trading society against the accurate, natural principle of love and kindness.

Granted, individuals are exposed to contradictory influences and a large panorama of teaching, but this antithesis at the very best would create neutrality. We add to this neutrality, a rebellious period in which children question most, if not all, of their values. The rebellion is generally followed by a more mature time of inventory. People ultimately pick and choose. A specific selection is made concerning which standards will remain or disappear. There must be some underlying feeling on which this choice is based. If a woman agrees that lying is wrong, there was something in herself that provided a comparison.

Meanwhile, let me bring attention to the fact that our very condemnation of certain evil societies also argues against "The Wolf Pack Theory," for according to Moral Relativists, whatever a society decides to do cannot be questioned. Why then do we morally renounce the gladiator games of ancient Rome or the slave-based economic system of the Pre-Civil War South? Are we not assuming a universal standard which transcends culture?

I once asked this question to a student who claimed that the conscience was a human invention to help society function.

"So then," I said, "You have no problem with the early slave states, for they got together as a culture and decided that there was nothing wrong with owning other human beings as property. In fact, the institution of slavery was very convenient, for it boosted the prosperity of the South."

Wanting to be consistent with his earlier point, the student finally said, "I suppose that would be true."

"Let's be clear," I said. "Let's make sure there is no misunderstanding. Are you saying for the record that there is nothing wrong with slavery so long as a society agrees that there is nothing wrong with it?"

"I guess I am saying that."

"I don't think you really feel that way. You are claiming that way now to win an argument, but if we had met in a different context and were merely discussing racism or politics apart from philosophy, there is no way you would assert that slavery can be justified in any situation."

"Sure I would."

"Really? O.K. Let's try an experiment. You are on your way to class. I want you to ask the professor for just one minute of class time before the lecture begins. I want you to look your fellow students in the eye and say to them (without telling anyone about the context of our conversation), 'I just want all of you to know something about me. I do not believe that there was anything wrong with slavery in the Pre-Civil War South because a certain culture had made a decision about morality, and I believe we should respect the varied opinions of all cultures.' Would you be willing to give that announcement?"

He looked at me for a second and then said in a very cocky voice, "Yeah! Yeah, I'll go say that."

"O.K., I'll be out here tomorrow with this same book table at 1:00pm. If you come back and tell me you made that statement, I won't call you a liar. I'll believe you."

We made the appointment. *I never saw him again.* I'll eat my hat if he made that statement. He discovered that day that he did indeed believe in the value of people, a value which would be impossible if life was an accident.

"O.K., I agree that life would have no real meaning if we are accidental. But what about theory B? Supposing the universe is eternally existent with a meaning inherent in itself? After all,

people refer to God as eternally existent. If God's meaning can be eternal, why can't the same be true of our universe?"

Would a timeless existence apart from God explain the conscience? Not at all. Rules do not float around a godless universe like alphabet soup. Ethics are not interwoven with inanimate objects or chemical reactions. There can be no such thing as a mindless moral principle because morality is bound up with personality. It is a running commentary on how personalities interact.

Speaking of human personality, it contradicts the idea of an eternal, godless, impersonal universe. Personality had to come from somewhere. Something had to always exist. You can't get something out of nothing. No one will argue this point. It doesn't take much stretch of the imagination to conclude such an obvious truth. Now then, if something had to always exist, this something had to be a thinking, feeling, sentient personality. If not, we would be at a loss to explain where personality came from.

"Personality could have evolved."

Evolution is only an unproven theory. Even if the theory is credible to you, consider the fact that there are many theistic evolutionists—scientists who believe that for things to be constantly evolving from a lower order to a higher order, some type of Supreme Being must be ushering life along according to a strategy. Charles Darwin himself believed in God and did not write *Origin of the Species* to disprove God's existence.[3] But if you are talking about an evolution that moves according to randomness and chance, we have a serious problem. Whatever the theories as to how many billions of years it took, you are still claiming that ultimately, the *personal* came from the *impersonal*. That makes no sense according to any logic I ever heard of. Also, an impersonal universe would have no meaning, leaving human life once again as an accident.

"Maybe we are all part of some eternal consciousness that is merely part of the universe."

One would ask how finite people received an eternal nature and entered an eternal universe. All human beings have origin as well as death—two obvious mortal qualities. If we want to suggest that the first humans did not have parents, we are either affirming that they were created or suggesting that they themselves were without a beginning. Either way, we have brought a God back into the picture. At the moment, we are trying to imagine life without that possibility.

"O.K., maybe not eternal people but perhaps an eternal underlying force of some sort. Maybe this unseen power holds the universe together and supplies meaning."

We would at once ask if this power has feeling and intellect. If not, where did feeling and intellect come from? We are suggesting chaos and accident again. A power that arranges things must do so according to a plan. Without the plan, there is no point to the arrangement. With the plan, we are back to a personal power, a creator of some quality. Let's face it: It really makes no sense to leave out God when discussing the meaning to life.

"But many seem to live sensible lives without even thinking about God."

This is quite true. People frequently take the heavy questions for granted and concentrate instead on surface living. I once asked a college student if he ever thought about the meaning of life on a deeper level than school, work, or socializing. He responded by saying, "What else is there?" The ability to ignore a question does not invalidate the answer.

THE NATURE OF GOD

"All this does is make an argument for some kind of God. That doesn't mean He's the God of the Bible."

A good case can be made for the biblical God, but only after we establish God's nature. When doing so, we will conclude that God (whoever or whatever He is) is loving and good.

"Loving and good? Didn't you leap to that conclusion rather hastily?"

We learn about an artist from his artwork. Does it not make sense that Creation would tell us a few things about God? How can we explain any noble human qualities apart from the Source of Life?

"But now you will checkmate your own argument. You stated earlier that we do not completely submit to our standards. Does our evil come from God as well?"

An excellent question. Man observes good and evil in himself and good and evil in the world. Life appears to be a paradise invaded. The world is both a wonderful place and a terrible place at the same time. On one hand, we can enjoy beautiful lakes, lavish forests and breathtaking sunsets. Unfortunately, we also witness blizzards, earthquakes, and fatal diseases. This contradictory tension is equally apparent in the human species. Just as people love and create, they hate and destroy. Quite a riddle indeed. Some would assume from this phenomenon that God is not totally good. Such a conclusion is very understandable, but the theory does not completely hold up. Remember, our conscience and intuition tell us that people *should* be good and that life *should* be good. Can we assume that we are better than our creator? Of course not. An inferior being does not invent a superior being. Maybe you never stopped to think about it, but a complaint about evil in relationship to God is simply another way of saying, "I'm a better person than God is." Our creator at the very least will realize the same things that we do. He is fully aware of "how life should be." As God, He is also in the supreme position to do something about this truth. In other words, the creator of all life will not act contrary to His own standards.

"Supposing the creator is both good and evil? After all, people are both good and evil. Is this not the most likely possibility? Or perhaps we have two co-creators, a good one and a bad one."

There is no principle beyond God. We already established the relationship between morality and personality. Good and evil are not entities in themselves. They are choices and thoughts. It makes no sense to say that God would choose evil and choose good at the same time. The inward awareness of accountability tells you that God expects people to live a certain way. This revelation is based on a divine decision. To say that God is also evil is to make God undecided in the standards He wanted to establish. This would invalidate any reason to hold men and women accountable. Why would God create a conscience that condemns murder if He were uncertain how He Himself felt about murder? It would be a contradiction for God to say that evil was occasionally preferable or justified. If such were the case, evil would not be evil. "Evil" would be an opinion. Your conscience points to an awareness of God's opinion regarding standards. Such an opinion is ultimate reality. As our Creator, He holds the sole authority to establish such ideas.

A co-creator is also an unlikely possibility. In such a case, neither being will have the exclusive claim to authentic judgment. If a co-creator decides that evil is permissible, people, as products of two divinities, will find themselves in a state of moral neutrality. This, once again, leads to relative rules and a confusing life.

We could also conclude that an "evil god" is not really evil. He is instead, a timeless being who chose a different code of ethics. As one of two eternal entities, his decision goes unchallenged. Since the "good god" is an equal, not a superior, even He must remain silent. Both gods will therefore confess a difference of viewpoint. At the first appeal to "common ground," they are acknowledging principles of a higher order. Since that cannot be, the gods concede a stalemate. There is no hope for the "correct standards." "Good" will never prevail. On what basis would the moral God communicate to His creatures that good *should* prevail unless He wanted to lie? And if He lied, He would not be good Himself. What would be the final result? Everlasting, frustrating chaos which forces us to abandon our earlier conclusion that life had meaning. For reasons already mentioned, this is not an option.

There is, of course, another obvious question to ask. For what possible reason would a good and evil God collaborate in Creation? A God who is truly good will never cooperate with evil.

In the final analysis, the only sensible explanation for your conscience is one God who made an unquestionable decision. We do not know why His nature desired such a choice.

"Even if we throw out the evil god, does that mean that there is only one, righteous eternal creator?"

It does, as a matter of fact. Two eternal beings agreeing on purpose and morality would have to appeal to higher principles, and higher principles, once again, cannot exist apart from personality. One God need not appeal to anything.

"Why assume that God is eternal? Couldn't a finite god have created a finite universe?"

Yes, possibly, but even if our "god" is not infinite, an eternal creator would still be out there somewhere. We established earlier that an eternal personality must exist. Once establishing an eternal God, we recognize the possibility that He created us directly. In fact, it becomes highly questionable why He would use a "middle man." Nevertheless, to maintain an open mind, we will simply conclude at this point that with or without a finite god, the infinite God is alive.

"Well, then, could our hypothetical finite creator be evil?"

Because the eternal God will not act contrary to His goodness, we assume that the finite god (if he exists), was created to be loving and good.

"But could not the 'finite god' have fallen into evil choices just as men and women did?"

Yes, potentially, but the infinite God, because of His nature would not let such a being hold His Creation accountable to standards He Himself doesn't even follow. For that would not be fair to the third party. Our moral imperfection can only be measured against the standard of moral perfection.

In summary, a finite creator, by contrast to the infinite Creator is not truly God, and our ultimate source of life, therefore, is the eternal God. It is this God to whom I refer for the rest of the chapter. Once God reveals more of Himself, He will let us know whether any kind of middle finite helper exists as well.

"But if morality was established by God, could I not disagree with His establishment?"

The question is irrelevant because you were created in such a way that you do not disagree. You disobey, but you do not disagree.

"But is this really goodness?"

Yes, because the author of life says so. There can never be a more final decision. Remember, there was a time when only God with His personality and morals existed. Since He created everything, it is impossible to find a legitimate basis with which to challenge Him.

FROM LOVE TO THE BIBLE

The establishment of a loving God supplies many additional conclusions because there are many things a loving God would do and many things a loving God would not do. We can now test different religions to see if they are indeed talking about a loving God.

I will define religion as "an alleged truth about our existence, revealed from some type of higher order." These various belief systems should be compared to the following expectations:

First of all, if the Creator is loving, the Creator will reveal Himself to people. I am frequently amazed at the typical assumption that God would be doing something out of the ordinary by speaking with His own Creation. Certainly God is capable of communication. Otherwise, we would not be capable either. Is it conceivable that a moral God would withhold such contact? Would it not be cruel for Him to create us for a reason and then not let us in on the secret? A search for meaning apart from some type of religion leads only to the dead end of despair. A loving God would not delight in such emptiness. If meaning and value are found only in the Creator, He would be most cold not to share this meaning and value. We must conclude that a loving God reveals Himself.

Our next question deals with the specifics of His revelation. *Naturally, we cannot place limitations on God's mode or style.* We should rid ourselves of ultimatums like the following: "If God has something to say to me, let Him contact me at exactly 2:00 a.m. He must appear on my living room TV screen and He must look just like George Burns!"

Is God obligated to accommodate our peculiar expectations? Not at all. God can communicate any way He chooses. It may be with an audible voice, but He could also use dreams, visions, prophets, feelings, all of the above, or none of the above. Remember, we are not inventing the rules.

We would also assume that if the Creator is revealing Himself to people, He has always been revealing Himself to people, for this too would be the only consistent act of love. I am quite suspicious of the "lone prophet" who claims to be the first person to ever "encounter God." Such partiality would be quite unfair to the billions who have been around since the beginning of time. With all due respect to divine activity, we have just eliminated most religions for consideration by disregarding all new ones! Only ancient religions are still in the running, provided they give claim to revelation as far back as human history can be traced. But there must be more than a claim. It makes sense that people would keep records of such divine activity. God's intervention generation after generation can hardly escape notice for it would have influenced history in dramatic and powerful ways. A collection of 39 ancient manuscripts known as the Old Testament makes such a claim. Judaism, Christianity, and Islam all adhere to the Old Testament. The scriptures of Hinduism and Native American traditions are examples (although, not exclusive examples) of alternate divine claims that also point to antiquity.

"If God is willing to speak with everyone, why are there so many different religions? Do they each present the same truth in a different fashion? If so, Jesus would not be the only way."

We are moving now into the question of consistency. It would help to start with a teaching of the ancient philosopher, Aristotle. I am referring to his Law of Non-Contradiction.[4] This law (foundational to philosophy) states that two given truth claims must not contradict. If they do, at least one of them is wrong and possibly they are both wrong. In other words, I can't call my wife on the phone and say, "I'm coming home for dinner and yet, I am not coming home for dinner." Sound simple? It should. We accept this idea without hesitation in every facet of life—every facet of life except religion, that is.

People are usually afraid to test religions out of fear that they will be showing intolerance. It should be noted that one can respect freedom of religion without assuming that all religions are equally valid, for such a conclusion is intellectually dishonest.

While lecturing at the University of Minnesota, the noted apologist Cliffe Knechtle was confronted by a student who claimed that all religions were basically the same. Cliff responded with a piercing analogy:

"If I were to assume that all Chinese people were the same," he said, "it would mean one of two things: either I'm a bigot, or I have not taken the time to get to know Chinese people. The same is true of religious assumptions."[5]

Even when admitting that religions do in fact teach opposite theologies, many stubbornly grasp the idea that somehow every one of them came from the same God. Why is it so easy to envision a creator who unveils contradictory information? *Why must a belief in God be divorced from our God-given ability to think?*

Paradoxically, people are not afraid to put Christianity through the ringer. Its claims are confronted all the time. Once while doing an open forum at Fresno City College, I was asked about Mormonism. I mentioned that Mormonism claimed to go by the Bible, yet taught polytheism,[6] which completely contradicts the Bible (Isaiah 43:10).

A young lady raised her hand and said, "What right do you have to stand here and scrutinize somebody else's religion?"

"Hold on," I replied. "For the last two hours you and your friends have been doing nothing but scrutinizing my religion. 'Doesn't the Bible contradict itself?' 'How do we know Jesus rose from the dead?' 'Why would a loving God send people to Hell?' etc. And this has not bothered me. It has been very appropriate. You *should* challenge anyone who makes a truth claim, but it works both ways. I will ask these same questions of other religions."

She nodded as her double standard became obvious. Her earlier skeptical questions confirmed an honest, inward conviction that all beliefs, even religious ones, must be examined. We must test whether they contradict themselves and we must test whether they contradict each other. There isn't space right now to give every major religion its rightful day in court, but some brief examples will at least illustrate the process.

Some Hindus believe that God and Creation are one and the same.[7] The Bible, on the other hand, paints a major distinction between the Creation and the Creator. If one person says, "God made the tree," while another says, "Actually, God is the tree," we cannot possibly conclude that they are both correct, even though they each use a similar word, *God*. Of course, this leads us to no conclusion at all about the accuracy of Hinduism or Christianity. It is instead a conclusion about the fallacy of Universalism (the belief that all religions are true). On the other hand, Hinduism makes no claims to historical verification and this is a significant thing to note.

There are also contradictions between religions which accept the Bible. Islam claims that in addition to the Koran, both the Old and New Testaments are the word of God.[8] Jesus is described in the Koran as a holy prophet, but not an incarnation of God Himself.[9] The test for a prophet in the Old Testament is that he must be accurate in everything he teaches (Deuteronomy 8:22). Jesus taught that He was God (John 14). If Jesus was lying, He was not a prophet, but Islam claims He was a prophet. If Jesus was telling the truth, then He is God. But Islam claims He wasn't God. Either way, we have a rather serious contradiction.

Judaism teaches that the Old Covenant will be changed after the Messiah comes (Jeremiah 31:31-34). Daniel 9 actually computes that time by measuring the amount in Hebrew years of thirty days each. He starts with the return of the Jews from Persian exile when King Artaxerxes freed the Jewish slaves, and ends with Messiah's arrival. This day occurred on Nisan 10 according to the Persian Calendar or March 30, 33 A.D. according to the Julian calendar.[10] Only one potential Messiah rode into Jerusalem that day—Jesus of Nazareth. If He was the Messiah, then Judaism's New Covenant (Christianity) is now in force. If He wasn't the Messiah, then Daniel was a false prophet. But Judaism considers Daniel to be a true prophet. We have found a contradiction with Judaism as well.

I must be making myself very unpopular right now. Please understand, I *do* respect the many Muslims, Hindus, Jews, Mormons, Universalists, and others I have met as honest and dedicated people. However, this does not keep me from examining their claims.

"But is Christianity any more consistent? It seems that there are many contradictions to the Bible."

Yes, it does seem that way. We must remember that the Bible was written in other languages by cultures far removed from ours. Most alleged contradictions stem from a misunderstanding of certain terms and phrases. For example, Jesus predicted that He would be in the grave for "three days and three nights" (Matthew 12:40). When we read the passion narratives we see that He was crucified late Friday afternoon and that He rose from the dead early on Sunday morning. It is impossible to get three days and three nights out of this, and I have seen many atheists refer to Jesus' prophecy as a "blatant error which completely destroys the credibility of the Bible."

The solution comes with an understanding of the way ancient Jews spoke. To a Jew, any part of a day was viewed as a whole day.[11] Describing part of a day as "a day and a night" may seem foreign to us, but that is because we live two thousand years later in a completely different culture. We must realize that if the Bible did not contradict itself to the original audience it was written for, it cannot contradict itself to us. This is only one example of the many apparent Bible contradictions that melt away in light of authentic historical interpretation.

"But the Old and New Testaments are very different. Isn't that a contradiction too?"

No, because again, the Old Testament predicts the new. The consistency we expect is not in the quantity of information but in the accuracy of the facts. For example, if Susan has a vision in which God says, "I love corporate worship," and Ron has a vision in which God says, "I love private worship," it is possible that both parties received an authentic vision. God may like both. But supposing Susan heard God say, "I hate corporate worship," while Ron heard, "I love corporate worship". Now somebody is on the wrong frequency. At least one person did not have a true encounter. After all, God is not schizophrenic.

Likewise, if God had warned the Hebrews to never expect another covenant from Him, then any prophet who claimed to institute a new agreement between God and man could be immediately labeled as false. But instead, God said through Jeremiah:

'Behold, the days are coming,' declares the Lord, 'when I will make a new covenant with the house of Israel and with the house of Judah, not like the covenant I made with their forefathers...' – Jeremiah 31:31-32

"If there is only one God who reveals Himself, how then, do we account for the differences in people's beliefs?"

A loving God would be a gentleman. He would not force Himself upon those who don't want Him, but would instead speak to those who are seeking. Most people accept the religion they were brought up in without question. Others, when choosing a religion, choose the one that they like or the one that is convenient. Sometimes, like sheep, they are mesmerized by talented orators who speak with charisma and authority. We have only to recall the 900 unfortunate individuals who followed Jim Jones into the wilderness, to remember that most become religious simply to have their needs and feelings satiated. Seldom do they say, "I will examine the evidence to see which (if any) of these religions is actually true."

"Disproving another religion doesn't prove Christianity. Neither does the harmonization of an alleged Bible contradiction prove the Bible."

That is true. Therefore, let us see what we should expect from an accurate religion and compare Christianity accordingly.

First of all, the religion will go hand in hand with our own conscience. This means that God will someday, somehow hold people accountable for the way they live. If He didn't, He would not be a just God. Justice is certainly one quality of goodness. This introduces an immediate problem. I am referring of course to our universal guilt. Because nobody lives a righteous life, our divine judge will have to condemn us all. Or will He? Nobody seems to be able to submit completely to the conscience. People are apparently trapped. Would there be no mercy to the woman who cries for release? Would there be no hope for the victim who hates his wicked nature and desires change? Mercy is never an obligation, but mercy is still a sophisticated quality found within the imperfect human. Again, would people have a worthy quality that God doesn't have? How can a loving God execute justice and mercy at the same time? How might He deliver people from the shackles of their own deadly selfishness? This is not an easy question to answer, but an accurate religion will address the puzzle.

We would also expect some religious teachings concerning life after death. The person who claims that death is final has a hard time supporting his remark. If death was final, God would be cruel. I say this for the simple reason that all people cherish a pleasant, enjoyable life. Who could ever wish for such contentment to end? It would have been less evil for God to abort His plan of Creation than to put us here with a love for life and then pull the plug, consigning us to oblivion without ever again having even a conscious thought.

"But some people are glad to die. Suffering in the world makes life miserable."

Granted. But these people would have preferred a fulfilling life. Otherwise, they would not view suffering as tragic. Even the person who commits suicide will do so because of depression or some tragedy she couldn't cope with. A tired weak, sick old woman might prefer death over her condition, but if it were possible, she would much rather be rejuvenated to experience, once again, the health and energy of her youth. The fact that we even die at all is certainly a mystery along with the origin of evil, but apparently people were not meant to die. Death is a slap in the face—a final disaster. A loving Father will provide some kind of solution for our sick world, a remedy that overcomes death. All forms of evil must someday be destroyed. What is only a hope to us is a future certainty to God.

"This doesn't prove the Christian belief in resurrections. There are other ideas about life after death, like reincarnation, for instance."

Reincarnation offers no hope from any honest practical perspective. If I am a reincarnated soul, I am completely unaware of my other lives. This means that should I die, and come back again, my future identity will be without knowledge of this life. As Bob Siegel, I perceive my present state as all that I know and love. If this should end, how can I receive consolation? My future existence as a new man (or woman) who does not remember Bob Siegel will be, for all intents and purposes, another person. How does this "hope" compare to the promise of living for all of eternity as the same person? The probability of reincarnation becomes highly questionable, especially in relationship to a caring Creator.

"But maybe there is another reason for reincarnation that is more important than our ability to remember. Maybe people are continually changing for the better each time they return."

Our species has had a long time to evolve. Show me the improvement. People are just as horrid and corrupt now as they were 10,000 years ago. As mentioned earlier, some of the worst atrocities were committed in the twentieth century. According to the suggestion of reincarnation, we have each completed thousands of lives. When will there be something to show for it?

"Some people claim to remember their past identities."

Some people claim to have received three magic wishes from a genie too. A rational improbability does not instantly change simply because of a claimed experience.

PLACING OUR TALL ORDER

It is time now to tie up the loose ends. What exactly are we looking for? An ancient religion with historical claims to consistent revelation from God. This loving God is both just and merciful. He will offer a deliverance from sin to those who crave such freedom. People who are content in their sin will still be held accountable. Along with this salvation, God will provide an explanation for evil in the world apart from His own activity. Finally, God will offer everlasting life in a paradise society free from corruption. In other words, we are looking for a God who shares the Gospel.

SUMMARY

The human conscience provides rational evidence for the existence of God. This same conscience suggests a loving deity. Such a God would reveal Himself to people and this revelation would not be new. We expect consistent communication from as far back as history can be traced. Embodied in this Scripture would be the hope of a resurrection, justice, mercy, and some kind of promise for the final elimination of evil. The only historical records which fulfill this expectation were eventually collected into one volume and entitled *The Bible*.

---

1 The Dubians of Dubu Island off the Southern shore of eastern New Guinea, have a rather unusual social system, one that people sometimes point to as evidence of a society which does not believe people should be respected. It seems, believe it or not, that the Dubians praise treachery and bad will. If, for example, one chooses to kill another, he should eat and drink with him first, so that the murder will seem especially traitorous. The Dubians have no chiefs, and no organization to speak of, but instead, live in virtual anarchy (Ruth Benedict, *Patterns Of Culture*, pp. 130-131).

It is important to note that the nearby neighbors of the Dubians consider them to be treacherous and the Dubians themselves, in order to praise treachery, are admitting in their own unusual way that treachery is evil. Their choice to willfully pervert standards does not disprove anything I have said about a universal knowledge of right and wrong.

2 The Supreme Court's fateful Dred Scott decision of 1857 ruled that black slaves were in fact non-human and therefore the property of their owners, even if they should escape and make their way to the North.

3 Although he still believed in God when he wrote *Origin of Species*, late in life Darwin had many doubts about the God of the Bible and considered himself to be an agnostic. This belief, however, still maintained that some kind of God might exist. Darwin stopped being a Christian partly because of the death of his daughter and not because of the theory of evolution alone (Rebecca Stefoff, *Charles Darwin and the Evolution Revolution*, Francis Darwin, *The Autobiography of Charles Darwin*, p. 61, 68 – 9).

Although I myself do not believe in the theory of evolution, it should still be pointed out that Genesis was not written as a science book, but rather as a history of the people of Israel. Only the first three chapters talk about the Creation of the world and the fall of human beings into sin. This tells us something about the priority of the writer. He was obviously giving a quick review of an oral tradition already known to the people. Only when Abraham comes on the scene in chapter 12 does the narrative slow down and begin to give intricate detail. We conclude that specifics about creation were not the writer's intention.

The first chapter of Genesis is written in a style of writing known as Hebrew Poetry. It is not seeking to give any kind of order to creation as evidenced by the fact that the world exists with water and vegetation prior to the creation of the sun (Genesis 1:14). The word for day (yom) is a Hebrew word that did not have to mean a literal 24 hour day but could also be referring to an event (Joel 1-3). This poem then, could simply be God's way of discussing different events in the stages of creation.

The Bible portrays God as being completely removed from time (2 Peter 3:8, Revelation 13:8). Time is a human limitation. When we ask whether it took God six days or six million years to create the world, the question is irrelevant. In fact, it took God no

amount of time at all to create the world because God does not exist in time. To speak at our level, God is using language we will relate to. Since we live in time and space, it is possible that a very long process over the years (as we understand years) created the world and slowly brought about different forms of life.

Genesis, then, leaves room for the theory of evolution or perhaps a better theory. I personally would put my emphasis on the words "perhaps a better theory" but for now, belief in an old earth along with Darwin's theories does not contradict the Bible in any way.

4 Aristotle, *Metaphysics* 1.v3.100 5b8-34.

5 I witnessed this conversation myself.

6 See *King Follet Discourse* published in the Mormon newspaper, *Times and Seasons* (Aug. 15, 1844, pp. 613-14).

7 See the *Bhagavad-Gita*, The Vision of God, p. 75, translation by Swami Prabhavananda and Christopher Isherwood, published by Barnes and Noble, 1995.

8 See *Koran* 2:174-77, 5:44-7, 65-70, 10:35-9.

9 See *Koran*, 5:70-74, 4:171-73.

10 For a full and scholarly treatment of this subject, see H.W. Hoehner, *Chronological Aspects in the Life of Christ*
(Zondervan Publishing House, Grand Rapids Michigan, 1977).

11 Rabbi Eleazar Ben Azariah (A.D. 100) says "A day and a night are an Onah (a portion of time) and the portion of an Onah is as the whole of it." (As quoted by H.W. Hoener, Ibid.).

Part Two: Moral Apologetics

Chapter 4

WHY DOES THE BIBLE CALL CERTAIN PRACTICES SINFUL?

"Why does the Bible call certain practices sinful? There are behaviors and lifestyles which do not seem wrong to me at all, and yet Christians condemn them simply because of certain Bible verses. I realize that if the Bible really is the Word of God, I would be foolish not to obey it. Still, it would help if once in a while God could explain why something is wrong instead of just saying, 'Because I said so.' None of us liked hearing that reason from our parents when we were kids, and it is a lame reason when it comes from God as well."

I think it is appropriate to ask God questions. True, some of what He reveals is a mystery, but morality seems to be one of the issues of which God has chosen to be abundantly clear. This makes sense since it is in the area of morality and ethics that God will hold us accountable.

THE ESSENCE OF SIN

I am going to make an outrageous claim. I am convinced that any standard found in the Bible is a standard every person will agree with. Deep inside the human conscience we each affirm the laws of the Bible. We may not all be obeying them, but we all agree with them.

"Come now. You can't be serious. I can think of several practices that many in our society condone but the Bible condemns. Look at the issues of premarital sex, abortion and homo – sexuality, just to name three controversial ones."

I am prepared to back up my smug claim. But first, we must define the word *sin*. When the Bible calls something *sinful* it is referring to *selfishness*. I do not mean positive self-esteem but rather any personal convenience that comes at somebody else's expense. Where do I get this definition? From Jesus, in his Sermon on the Mount:

> *In everything, do to others what you would have them do to you. For this sums up the Law and the Prophets. – Matthew 7:12*

This simple yet profound teaching, (sometimes referred to as the Golden Rule) is intended as a summary of the entire Mosaic Law. Jesus is talking about the Old Testament, but in those days they did not yet use the term *Old Testament*. They used the term *Scriptures or Law and the Prophets*. Earlier in this very same sermon, Jesus had said:

> *Do not think that I have come to abolish the Law and the Prophets. I have not come to abolish them, but to fulfill them. – Matthew 5:17*[1]

If sin is described in the Bible as the breaking of God's law (Romans 6), and if God's law is summed up as a command to treat people *unselfishly*, then *selfishness* is the resulting definition of sin. Once we have defined sin as selfishness, it is much more difficult for people to say that they disagree with the Bible's standards because in actuality we are talking about only one standard.

> *The entire law is summed up in a single command: 'Love your neighbor as yourself'* (Galatians 5:14, Apostle Paul referring to another statement of Jesus in which He said the same thing in a different way).[2]

Few people are going to claim that they object to such a moral imperative. Other religions and even nonreligious philosophies such as Humanism or Atheism ascribe to the basic notion of treating others with respect. Observe the clear relationship between the Golden Rule and the Ten Commandments: If I really love my neighbor, I will not steal from him, I will not sleep around with his wife and, of course, I will not kill him.

"Yes, those are obvious examples. But there are other practices condemned in the Bible which don't seem to have anything to

do with selfishness."

The relationship between biblically-labeled taboos and selfishness is not always immediately apparent. But if we can find the connection, we can agree with God's appraisal of the action. Although we could explore many examples to illustrate this theme, I will limit myself to three of the most difficult ones, subjects that come up frequently today and which were mentioned earlier— premarital sex, homosexuality and abortion.[3]

Since all three practices relate to human sexuality, sex in general is a good place to start.

PRE-MARITAL SEX

A student once approached my book table at the University of California at San Diego, claiming that the Bible was outdated. He mentioned the listing of certain sexual sins as an example. Certainly he could see the betrayal and dishonesty associated with adultery, but sex outside of marriage was another story. He acknowledged that the Bible labeled premarital sex as a sin (1 Corinthians 7:1), but expressed bewilderment as to why it was a sin. After I asked him if he at least agreed with Jesus' Golden Rule he quickly said, "Yes, of course."

"So we would both agree that we should treat others the way we want to be treated?" "Sure. But that has nothing to do with sex."

"Supposing I could show you that it did?" I asked.

"I doubt that you could. Tell me," he continued, "what's wrong with having sex with my girlfriend as long as I love her?"

"Nothing," I said.

The student almost fell over with astonishment. "What?"

"Nothing," I repeated.

"Nothing?"

"Nope. If you love her, as you say, nothing is wrong with having sex."

It was clear that he was unprepared for this answer. He had obviously expected me to quote some Bible verses that slammed pre-marital sex.

"Wow. I must admit. You're more open-minded than most Christians I meet."

"Well, I'm not done yet."

His cheery disposition melted as he awaited an explanation that would surely show the "fine print."

I continued. "When you say you love your girlfriend, what do you mean?"

"Huh?"

"What do you mean exactly when you say you love your girlfriend? We both seem to agree to a certain standard here that sex belongs in the context of love. That is fine, but how are you defining love?"

"I don't know…I love her. That's all."

"Is this love just a feeling or does it include a commitment?"

"Well…I'm committed to her."

"For how long? Are you committed for life? Do you love her unconditionally? Or do you only love her until someone more attractive comes along, or until you grow tired of her or until she displays some weakness that you don't want to live with? Are you willing to someday leave her, this woman with whom you became so intimate, this person who made herself so vulnerable to you as she expressed her sexuality? Could you someday desert her and devastate her by breaking her heart?"

In only a few short moments, this poor student realized that he didn't love his girlfriend nearly as much as he thought he did. But isn't it interesting to see that even without a Bible, he did have some standards in relation to sexuality. Sex, apart from love, was wrong. This he could understand. This he could relate to.

God is not some celestial killjoy who gets upset when we are having a good time. God is not anti – sex. God invented sex. A whole book in the Bible, *Song of Solomon*, is nothing but a sensuous love sonnet between a man and a woman.[4] But God *does* care about broken hearts. God is interested in the way we treat people. For these reasons He speaks against sex outside of marriage.

"O.K.," the student continued. "Supposing I were to decide never to leave her. I will never break up. Then can we have sex?"

"Well," I responded, "If you are really committed to her for life and vice versa, then we are talking about marriage. That's what marriage is, so this would not be sex outside of marriage but sex within marriage."

"Yeah, but what if we wanted to be committed without legally marrying?"

"What would be your reason for that? Is your relationship with her a secret? Are there certain people whom you don't want to know about it? If you can't be open about your commitment to her, it isn't really a commitment. Other women will still feel free to flirt with you and men with her."

"O.K.... Well...we don't have to make it a secret. But, why is a marriage license so important? Isn't the main thing that we are committed before people and before God? Why is a piece of paper such a big deal?"

"The piece of paper *isn't* a big deal. The main thing is being committed before people and before God. So, since you have done that and since the marriage license isn't a big deal anyway, why not just go ahead and get a marriage license? After all, it is only putting on paper the reality of your situation."

I wish you could have been there to see the look on his face. Obviously, one who is not ready for a marriage license is one who has not truly made a marriage commitment. Perhaps if some couple were stranded on a desert island committed to each other, they could have sexual relations provided they truly take a vow before God, promising Him that if they ever get rescued, they will obtain a marriage license immediately. But this student didn't fall into such a category. He came to realize that we weren't making wedding rings, pieces of paper or even Bible verses into something sacred in their own right. Instead, we were discussing a God who looks at our hearts and motives and gives us this one command: "As you would have people treat you, treat them."

Another student once asked me a similar question, but he left out words such as *love* and *commitment* finding them unnecessary. "What is wrong with sleeping around with women?" he asked. "I am not hurting anybody. Maybe our sexual relations are casual. Maybe these women won't mind me leaving them eventually or having a one-night stand. So, again, what harm is being done?"

Notice how he did agree that sex would be wrong if harm *were* being done. He just didn't see the harm. Of course he did find it necessary to make some immediate qualifications. If venereal diseases were transmitted, certainly that would be harm, and if he got a woman pregnant certainly that would say something about the need to associate sex with commitment. But my cheery friend was quite confident that he could have free, safe sex without incurring such results.

"Tell me then, what is wrong with pre-marital sex?"

"Nothing is wrong with the experience itself," I answered. "God isn't upset that you enjoy women, but these women may someday be married to husbands who would object to what you did. Can you relate to these men? Let me ask you a question: Supposing you had just been

80

married and on your honeymoon night your wife turned to you and said, 'Sweetie, I have a confession to make. I slept around with fifty men before I met you.'"

He gave a sly grin, "Obviously that would bother me. But come on, fifty men? Isn't that kind of an exaggeration?"

"O.K. forty…Feel better now? How about just ten? Just five?"

He finally admitted to me that he would feel bad even if his wife-to-be had only slept with one man.

"So what are you saying here?" he complained. "Am I not supposed to get married to a woman who has a past? I thought the Gospel was about forgiveness."

"Of course it's about forgiveness," I said. "And we all have a past. But you weren't asking me about forgiving a violation of the standard. You were simply asking if the standard exists. And it certainly does. We both agree that we should treat others the way we want to be treated. Sleeping around with women, even women who say they are uninterested in a commitment from you, is unfair to the way their future husbands may feel. You are not showing those future husbands the respect you would have wanted your wife's previous suitors to show you. Therefore, Jesus' Golden Rule applies again."

A third challenge came from the hardest nut to crack. Asking him a similar question, I received a completely different answer. "Honestly?" he said, "I would not care if my wife had slept with fifty men or a hundred men before she met me."

I wasn't sure I believed him. I wasn't sure if he had ever truly fallen in love and experienced that small emotion called jealousy. Still, I took him at his word and went on.

"But whether or not it bothers you, future husbands of the women you sleep around with may be bothered."

"That's their problem!" he snapped.

"No, that's your problem if you are going to take Jesus' words seriously, 'As you would have people treat you, treat them.' You should respect their feelings, and they in turn should respect yours, even when you feel differently about things."

HOMOSEXUALITY

"All this does, so far, is make a case for monogamy. What about homosexuals (called sinful in Romans I), who are willing to get married and be committed to each other? Certainly there is no harm being done there."

Yes, there is—psychological harm. I do not say this to sound condemning or to make anyone feel unwarranted guilt, but the truth is, people are involving themselves in a process that is unnatural. This was the widespread teaching of the American Psychiatric Association prior to the year 1973. Many people are unaware of the circumstances which led to homosexuality being declassified as an emotional disorder by the APA. You may never have heard about the pressure from gay activists and gay psychiatrists who were involved in the meetings. You should know that the discussions leading to the vote were not characterized with scholarly study but rather a great deal of fear. In fact, so extended was the pressure, that only one third of the ballots sent out were ever returned. Out of those returned, only 58 percent agreed to declassify homosexuality as a mental disorder. Get that? Fifty – eight percent out of the one third returned or about 19 percent overall! [5]

Prior to this time, homosexuals not only sought help from psychologists, but received healing. Dr. Charles Socarides, who had successfully treated gays for more than 20 years said that the militant gay movement was responsible for "the greatest medical hoax of the century."[6]

Although many gay people sincerely claim that they cannot remember a time when they weren't attracted to the same sex, that does not necessarily mean they were born homosexuals. Elizabeth Moberly, a research psychologist for Oxford and Cambridge, explains this by pointing out that people absorb their key influences of sexual orientation between the ages of two and five, a time in life most of us would not remember anyway.[7]

Even molecular biologist Dean Hamer of the National Cancer Institute, who headed one of the famous studies which sought to find genetic explanations said, "Our studies try to pinpoint the genetic factors, not to negate the psychosocial factors."[8]

It may someday be discovered that there are two types of homosexuality, a learned behavior and a genetic predisposition. In either case, the homosexual in all likelihood did not choose his/her sexual orientation and should not be blamed for inward feelings or impulses. Likewise, in either case, the acting out of such impulses would still be unnatural behavior. It is believed that one can be born with a predisposition toward alcoholism too, but we would not encourage an alcoholic to drink.

"If homosexuality is really so unnatural, how come most people don't view it that way?"

Actually, I am convinced that most people do. They have trouble admitting this because of today's political climate, which has been growing now for over three decades.

I went to high school in the early seventie,s coming out of a home so sheltered that for years I had never even heard of homosexuality. When I discovered that certain fellow actors in my high school drama department were gay, my initial response was one of repulsion, despite the fact that they were very nice people. Of course, in a theater atmosphere people quickly learn to dismiss such feelings as rigid and old-fashioned. So, in no time at all I decided that varying sexual lifestyles must be respected. There was no room for judgment and backwoods thinking. In hindsight, it is interesting to note that my first reaction had nothing to do with the Bible because I wasn't even a Christian or Bible believer at the time. I was merely making a simple, obvious observation that men were meant for women and vice-versa. Still, in time, it was easier to accept the idea that my feelings were outdated than to consider the possibility that the majority opinion may be mistaken.

But what does the majority really think? That is the interesting question. Have you ever seen a sitcom where two men danced or one man accidentally kissed another? We see it all the time. It's a common device and we laugh all the time. It's an easy guaranteed laugh. Consider the finale of *Cheers*. Two gay lovers were in the middle of a quarrel when one pleaded with his partner calling him by the pet name "Muffin." The audience laughed hysterically and I'm sure the producers felt that this was a very progressive episode because of a willingness to portray gay romance as normal. One question: Why did people laugh? Why did the writers obviously intend for people to laugh? What is funny about a man calling his lover "Muffin?" If indeed we recognize the normality of that relationship, what exactly strikes us as humorous?

Centuries ago, Hans Christian Anderson illustrated the value of a simple childlike mind. Remember his story *The Emperor's New Clothes*? A charlatan tailor wanting to rook the king of a fortune, fashioned him a set of "fine apparel." There was one stipulation: Only intelligent people could see these clothes. Of course the clothes didn't really exist, so nobody ever really saw them. But nobody wanted to be viewed as unintelligent either. "If I can't see the clothes" one reasoned to himself, "the problem must be with me. After all, everyone else sees them."

You remember the rest. At a grand parade, one small child tugged at his mother's skirt and said, "But Mommy, he's not wearing any clothes."

Nakedness was once nakedness. Now, as the result of one clever tailor, the word "naked" in relation to the king was politically incorrect.

Could this same tailor have visited the United States? Maybe what we need today is an innocent child, like the one in the fairy tale; some red-faced, nose-running kid who hasn't studied genetics, hasn't studied psychology, hasn't studied Scripture and hasn't had sensitivity training. All he knows is what he sees and feels. Maybe if something looks unnatural it is unnatural. Maybe we all know the truth and are afraid to admit it. Maybe the king *isn't* wearing any clothes.

For what it is worth, I do believe that the Church has done a great disservice to the gay community by isolating this lifestyle as though it were more sinful than anything else. Although homosexuality is listed in Romans 1 as a practice God considers wrong, we must keep in mind that arrogance, jealousy, and gossip are also listed as sin. If the Church spent half as much time preaching against these practices as it does homosexuality, perhaps gay men and women could find a sanctuary.[9] How refreshing it would be if Christians could show sympathy for their struggles. Most gay people have already experienced much persecution, confusion, and alienation from others. By contrast, they should find a home in the church. After all, it is possible to accept people without condoning their sin.

A few years ago in Flagstaff, Arizona, a student approached me after one of my campus presentations: "I really like some of the things you said, but I have a question… Actually, I have a friend who is gay but is also curious to learn more about Christianity. He would like to attend a Bible Study, but he is afraid."

I suspected that we were not really talking about his friend, but I allowed him to continue. He explained the interest but also the reservations his "friend" had about visiting the local campus Christian fellowship.

"Well," I said, "I can understand his hesitation. I can also assure you that the Christian group sponsoring me today is a very open and loving community of people. They do not put on masks of spirituality. Instead, they are honest and down-to-earth. They will accept your friend as a fellow struggling sinner and they will not view him as a weird or second-class citizen."

He stared at me like a lost child looking for his parents, so I added,

"This I can promise you."

Tears rolled down the student's cheeks, and it became very obvious that he was talking about himself.

What saddened me is that although everything I told him about this particular Christian fellowship was true, in many places and at many churches I would not have been able to offer such assurance. But assurance, healing and forgiveness is what all people should find in Jesus.

The debate about whether homosexuality causes psychological harm will not be settled in these pages, but I'm sure the reader will agree that if such is the case, Jesus' Golden Rule applies again, for harm is harm whether it is emotional, physical, or psychological.

ABORTION

"How does the Golden Rule apply to abortion? Certainly birth control harms nobody and is solely the mother's business."

If abortion were only a matter of birth control, then I would completely agree. Once while participating in a panel discussion on abortion at UCSD, I heard a pro-choice panelist begin with a common disclaimer. "We all agree that abortion is a tragedy," she said, "but we must still protect the rights of women to make such decisions themselves."

I asked her a very simple question: "Why is it a tragedy? If this fetus isn't a life, if this is really just a bunch of tissue, then abortion isn't a tragedy, but rather another form of birth control."

I think it is obvious that abortion applies to the Golden Rule quite easily. *It is selfish and therefore wrong to take an innocent life.* Period. Nobody will argue that point. They may argue about whether or not abortion is in fact killing. They may claim that the fetus is not a life, but we would all agree that if abortion is the taking of a human life, then it is wrong because killing is wrong. This has nothing to do with any kind of spiritual belief about the soul or the afterlife. This has nothing to do with imposing a religious creed upon a society that embraces separation between Church and State. Instead, we have established common ground: Whether Christian, atheist, or otherwise, killing is killing.

"Yes but just because the Bible says that the fetus is a life (Luke 1:39-45) that doesn't mean medical science agrees."

Actually, medical science does agree.[10] *The only disagreements have to do with judgment calls entitled "quality of life."* In his novel 1984 George Orwell predicted a time when we would change our speech to nullify the effects of our actions. *1984* has arrived. In fact, this Newspeak has been here so long, it has turned into the 2000s, and it will go far into the twenty-first century.

Some time ago, to place emphasis on the truth that abortion is nothing less than the taking of a human life, Right to Life activists came up with a suitable term to describe their position—"Pro-Life." Advocates of abortion found a strategy of their own by dubbing themselves "Pro-Choice." This is understandable. After all, we didn't expect them to call themselves "Pro-Death." *Death* is a horrible word. *Choice* is a nice word. To say that you are against choice is to deny the constitution and its protection of individual rights.

Of course, Pro-Lifers also claim concern for rights. If, in fact, the unborn fetus is a human being, what could be a more atrocious assault to freedom and dignity than the destruction of a baby?

"Baby?" the pro-choicer shouts with anger. "Why, that's no baby. It's a fetus."

Yes, it's a fetus. *Fetus*, you'll be interested to know, is the Latin word for "little one." *Fetus* means *baby*. Abortion means "termination of the fetus." *Termination* means *kill*. And so class, "termination of the fetus" is Orwellian for "kill the baby." Since Orwellian seems a classier language than English, many wish to keep speaking Orwellian. That way no person will feel the impact of what they are truly talking about.

But Orwell predicted another way of disguising an issue: the re-writing of history. Here is the new history of the Right to Life movement: "You see, it never had anything to do with concern for the unborn. Instead, a bunch of male chauvinist pigs who wanted to eternally suppress women sat around a big coffee table and decided that they were against all forms of birth control. Any man who denies a woman this fundamental right is against feminism in any form. He wants to see all women submissive to their husbands, rustling up grub in the kitchen." That is our new history of the abortion controversy; a clever re-writing of the fact that most of the leaders in the Pro – Life movement are women.[11] This is not a man versus women issue. This is an issue women themselves are split over, even women feminists. In fact, there is an organization called *Feminists for Life*, made up of people who care about the rights of all females, including unborn baby girls.[12]

The re-writing of history continues. Pro-choicers point to the victims of rape and incest as the dominant reasons for keeping abortion legal. What was carefully whited out this time? The fact that very few abortions are done for those kinds of reasons.[13] Many Pro-Life people (including myself) believe that rape and incest are special cases. We may counsel a victim to consider the fact that an unborn human life is still at stake, but we would be very sympathetic if she still chose an abortion.

One more re-write: Pro-Lifers are frequently called a lot of ridiculous names such as Fascist. Somehow today, anything conservative is likened to Fascism. Please remember that when Hitler brought the real Fascism (or a form of it called Nazism) to Germany, it was a very new trend for the Germans. If we really want to evaluate ideologies to see if they remind us of things Hitler stood for, let's take a look at people like Margaret Sanger, the founder of Planned Parenthood, who believed in superior breeding, approved of Hitler's early sterilization program,[14] and advocated forced sterilization for those whom she considered unworthy to produce.[15] Sanger even published an article by Dr. Ernst Ruldin, director of the Nazi medical experimentation program, in her journal *Birth Control Review*![16]

A time may come when the new language and new history are no longer needed. Some pro – abortionists would like to see the day when abortion is as mandatory in the U.S. as it already is in China.[17] If that day ever arrives, all the Pro-Choice rhetoric will be out the window, having outlasted its usefulness. There will be no more choice for mother or daughter. But I'm confident we will have some new Orwellian lingo to smooth it over such as "necessary sacrifice for the good of society as a whole." I fear that 1984 is going to be a very long year.

I realize that most women, when they have an abortion, do not think of it as murder. In my zeal to call actions what they truly are, I do not want to make a harsh accusation either. It may be sad that our society has learned how to justify this practice, and I am convinced that doctors who perform abortions realize just exactly what they are doing, but a young, frightened pregnant woman, led to believe (for whatever reasons) that abortion is just another form of birth control is not a cold-blooded killer and should not be labeled such. God looks at the heart and the motives. Even when motives show an eagerness to do the convenient thing and look the other way, God still forgives.

On the other hand, it is not impossible for people to peer beyond clichés or disguised words and admit that abortion is the taking of a human life. As a matter of fact, many of today's Pro-Life advocates are people who at one time had abortions themselves or who were prominently "Pro – Choice." Three very interesting individuals representing this changed position are Norma McCorvey, plaintiff in the famous Roe vs. Wade case that led to the Supreme Court's 1973 ruling to legalize abortion, Sandra Cano, plaintiff of the companion case, Doe vs. Dalton and Bernard Nathanson, an outspoken doctor who founded the National Abortion Rights Action League and who performed abortions himself.[18]

SUMMARY

Every human conscience agrees with God's standards as set forth in the Bible because it is really only one standard, a standard easy to affirm: "As you would have people treat you, treat them." To demonstrate whether or not an action is sinful, we must show how the action is selfish. It is selfish to harm people and harm knows many varieties, from the obvious harm of hurting or killing to the subtler emotional and psychological harm.

---

1 There were two types of laws given to the Israelites from God, through Moses. There was the Moral Law and the Ritual Law. Between each set, a kind of check and balance system existed. People, when breaking the Moral Law, could be forgiven by obeying the Ritual Law. The rituals included an elaborate system of offerings and animal sacrifices. It was believed that the blood of the animals atoned for the violation of God's ethical rules. Such commands as "Do not kill," "Do not steal," "Do not commit adultery," represent the Moral Law. If one broke a Moral Law but at least received atonement through a Ritual Law, God would consider that to be adequate obedience, even though in reality these people needed forgiveness just like the people of the New Testament era.

How then, did Jesus fulfill the law? In two ways: 1) His ultimate sacrifice and atonement for sin on the cross fulfilled the Ritual Law and 2) As a result of the forgiveness offered on the cross Jesus now sends the Holy Spirit to indwell us, thus fulfilling the Moral Law.

"But I tell you the truth: It is for your good that I am going away. Unless I go away, the Counselor will not come to you; but if I go, I will send Him to you. When He comes; He will convict the world of guilt in regard to sin and righteousness and judgment" (John 16:7-8).

The indwelling Holy Spirit magnifies our conscience and brings us into a relationship with God so personal that we find it harder and harder to ignore the inner voice which condemns our selfishness. The result is that we no longer need an external moral code because God has placed His law into our heart. Such a status is predicted by the prophet Jeremiah as a fulfillment of the Old Covenant and an ushering in of the new.

*"The time is coming," declares the Lord, "When I will make a new covenant with the house of Israel and with the house of Judah. It will not be like the covenant I made with their forefathers, when I took them by the hand to lead them out of the land of Egypt, because they broke my covenant even though I was a husband to them," declares the Lord. "This is the covenant I will make with the house of Israel after that time," declares the Lord. "**I will put my law in their minds and write it on their hearts…**" (Jeremiah 31:31-33).*

In summary: Jesus has fulfilled the Ritual Law by His death on the cross and the Moral Law by His imparting of the Holy Spirit. The Spirit guides us and inspires us to follow the one law God commands people to obey: the Golden Rule, Jesus' words from the Sermon on the Mount that tell us to make loving decisions and consider the feelings of others.

2 In Matthew 22:37-40, Jesus is asked what the greatest commandment is. He responds by saying,

'Love the Lord your God with all your heart and with all your soul and with all your mind.' This is the first and greatest commandment. And the second is like it: 'Love your neighbor as yourself.' All the Law and the Prophets hang on these two commandments.

These two commands are evidently so interrelated in Jesus' mind that He refers to the second as the summary of both back in Matthew 7:12. In each of these passages He is offering a condensed view of the Law and the Prophets. Apparently the love

for God is assumed if we love our neighbor and vice versa. Therefore, Jesus could describe this phenomenon as one command or two interchangeably. Paul seems to interpret Jesus that way when he cites the second commandment as being the single summary of the law in Galatians 5:14. Later, John ties it all together for us:

If anyone says 'I love God,' yet hates his brother, he is a liar. For anyone who does not love his brother whom he has seen, cannot love God whom he has not seen. And He has given us this command: Whoever loves God must also love his brother" (1 John 4:20-21).

3 The latter two topics are real hot potatoes. They invoke a great deal of emotion and tend to take on a life of their own thus immediately eclipsing any other Bible-related subjects. Therefore, to avoid getting sidetracked, I will discuss abortion and homosexuality very briefly in this book. To give those discussions the details they deserve, I have written lengthier pieces which the reader can study at another time. For a detailed look at abortion from this author, see *Pandora's Child*, and *The Last Windmill*. For a detailed look at homosexuality from this author, see *Closets, Kings, and Other Points of View.*

4 It is common for many pastors to interpret *Song of Solomon* as an allegory of Christ's love for the church. This view goes back to the time of early Christianity (See Origen's commentary of the Song) which in turn was influenced by a popular rabbinic view from ancient Judaism where the text was taken to mean "God's love for Israel." Prior to the Hellenistic era, Jews would have seen the text for what it was, a sonnet describing the love between a husband and wife. We know that Philo (20BC-54AD), a lover of both Judaism and Greek philosophy, made the Greek allegorical method popular.

Physical pleasure was considered unspiritual in many Greek philosophies and therefore, the Jews, now under a similar impression, sought to explain how this "unspiritual" but traditional book had found its way into their collected Scriptures. The answer seemed obvious: *Song of Solomon* must not really be talking about sex, not if it is correctly interpreted. (See *The Mishnah Tractate Yadaim 3:5*, for the commentary of Rabbi Akiba who was martyred 135 AD and who participated in the Council of Jamnia. See also *The Targum to the Song of Songs*.) I am comfortable taking the Scripture at face value prior to the Greek influence of Judaism. There is no reason to assume that human sexuality is an inappropriate topic for inclusion in the Bible.

5 See, Jeffrey Sakinover M.D. *Homosexuality and the Politics of Truth*; Ronald Beyer, *Homosexuality and American Psychiatry: The Politics of Diagnosis*, 1981, p. 101-54; Joseph P. Gudel, *"Homosexuality Fact or Fiction"*, *Christian Research Journal*, (Summer 1992) p. 30.

6 Dr. Charles Socarides, *Overcoming Homosexuality* (New York, 1980) p. 5.

7 For a full study of her views, see Elizabeth Moberly, *Homosexuality, A New Christian Ethic* (Attic Press, 1982).

8 *Time Magazine*, Nov. 13, 1995.

9 Homosexuality is not being isolated in the book either. Gossip, arrogance, and jealousy, although just as sinful, are not practices which are defended today by anyone and thus did not suit my present purpose: to discuss three practices that people have a difficult time seeing as selfish.

10 For a list of medical appraisals see Randy Alcorn, *Pro-Life Answers to Pro-Choice Arguments*, (1992), pp. 39-41.

11 61% of women are pro-life as opposed to 53% of men. *Wirthlin*, January 1998. The largest pro-life organization in America is *National Right to Life*. Nearly two thirds of *National Right to Life* are women. (John Wilke, *"The Real Women's Movement,"* *National Right To Life News*, (Dec. 14) p. 3).

12 This organization was founded in 1972. For more information, contact *Feminists for Life*, 733 15 St. NW Suite 1100, Washington D.C., 20005

13 1% of abortions are performed on women who are victims of rape or incest (*Alan Guttmacher Institute*). 1% of abortions are performed on women whose lives are in danger (*Center for Disease Control*).

14 L. Stoddard, *Into the Darkness, Nazi Germany Today*, p. 196. See also, Leon Whitney, "Selective Sterilization," Birth Control Review (June 1933), for an article endorsed by Sanger, praising the race purification programs of the Third Reich.

15 Margaret Sanger, "Plan for Peace," *Birth Control Review* (April, 1932).

16 Dr. Ernst Rudin, *"Eugenic Sterilization, An Urgent Need,"* Birth Control Review (April, 1933).

17 For more information about this viewpoint and other agendas found in the Pro-Choice movement, see George Grant,
Immaculate Deception (Northfield Publishing, Chicago, Illinois, 1996).

18 Operation Rescue, *National Annual Survey,* Nov. 1997.

Chapter 5

WHY WOULD A LOVING GOD SEND PEOPLE TO HELL?

"How can a loving God send people to Hell? The very idea of ongoing eternal torture is absolutely preposterous. Such uncivilized behavior makes God less loving than human beings, for what parents would banish their children forever?"

Of all the biblical doctrines, this one bothers people the most and with very understandable reasons. Nothing seems more vindictive than punishment from which there is no release. In Chapter 4, I suggested that deep inside, people actually agree with the standards of God as set forth in the Bible, even though such agreement is not always conscious or obvious. If this is true, it must also apply to the unpopular notion of Hell.

A MATTER OF JUSTICE

I am going to discuss Hell in a rather roundabout way by first bringing up another major question frequently asked about God: "How can a loving God allow suffering and evil in the world?" If we were to make a top ten list of "God" questions, this one would certainly be found on the high part of the chart close to the subject of Hell. Now, here is what's interesting: *These two separate concerns actually contradict each other.*

Years ago, at UC Santa Barbara, a foot patrol police officer who worked for the campus surrounding college community approached me on my way to our weekly large group Christian meeting. Since I was walking and not driving, it was the first time I was ever stopped by a cop without feeling nervous. As a matter of fact, he seemed to be the uncomfortable one. This husky, uniformed fellow had visited our meeting once before as a guest sitting quietly in the back of the auditorium. Since I had been the speaker that night, he recognized me .

today. His greeting was polite but intense. As we walked together, it became obvious that something important was on his mind. Finally the police officer spoke up. "You know…I just gotta say this. There are two reasons I can't believe in your God."

"Go on," I said.

"First of all, I cannot believe in a God who would send people to Hell. Secondly, I find it impossible to accept a God who could just sit around and watch the suffering of our world without doing something about it."

"Sir," I said, "are you aware that one of your objections actually answers the other? On one hand you object to a God who would sit back passively and not hold people accountable for the evil in the world. On the other hand, you object to the teaching which says that God *will* in fact hold people accountable."

I continued by reminding him that we had actually met a long time ago before he even visited our fellowship. The woman next door to my house called the police because her husband was beating her. As her drunk and screaming husband sat handcuffed in the police car, this very kind officer actually pleaded with the wife. "Ma'am, will you please, please file charges this time? It's always the same. Your husband beats you and you call the police. We come to your house, pick him up and bring him to jail. Then you come down to the station and drop the charges. A few weeks later he beats you again and you call us again. We've gone through this about seven times now. You make my job very difficult because I care about you, and I'm afraid that one of these evenings you are going to turn up dead! Your husband is dangerous! He isn't going to change! He needs to be locked up!"

When I witnessed that conversation, I remember thinking about how compassionate this police officer was, how he went beyond the call of duty out of genuine, heartfelt concern. Talking to him now, a year later, I commended him for this and reminded him that he was made in the image of God, His personality and His convictions.

Our earthly court systems reveal how we honestly feel about a heavenly court system. After all, if a human judge were to let a murderer or rapist go free, would we not view him as a reckless and irresponsible judge? In fact, would he not also be an unloving judge to put so many innocent people at risk with his careless decision? Likewise, what kind of judge would God be if He didn't hold people accountable for the way they lived their lives? What kind of community would Heaven be if God permitted evil people to live there? If sin were not removed from paradise, it wouldn't be much of a paradise. We must think of Hell as a prison, which separates out wicked people, preventing them from doing harm to others. When viewed this way, Hell paints the picture of a just, and therefore loving God.

Imagine a man like Hitler, who after the extermination of millions of innocent people, took a few capsules and died a quick death so that the allied armies on their way to Berlin could never take him to justice. Isn't there some measure of consolation in the belief that Hitler will actually have to stand accountable before God? Doesn't it feel good to know that evil people will not really get away with anything and that good will ultimately prevail?

> **"I can accept the idea of accountability, but isn't eternal punishment rather drastic? After all, we aren't talking about selected evil people deserving Hell but rather, all people, according to your Christian Gospel. O.K., we are imperfect, but do we really deserve the same fate as those who actually commit murder?"**

Jesus internalized the Ten Commandments. To Him, even having the instinct of a murderer was a serious problem, whether we actually commit the crime or not (Matthew 5:21- 22). Quite frankly, we have grown so accustomed to our "normal everyday sin" that we don't view it the way God does. We may be aware that certain thoughts or actions are wrong, but their utter repulsion is something we have difficulty seeing.

When I was in college, I had a part-time job at a convalescent home—one that was not very well kept up. The first day I arrived, I felt as though I wanted to stop breathing because there was a horrible stench. For about a week, I dreaded coming to work. As time went on, the stench bothered me less until eventually I couldn't even smell it anymore. But this was not because the smell ever went away. Instead, I had actually gotten used to it. We get used to our sins too.

Eternal punishment may still seem drastic. It's certainly drastic to God. Why else would He have sent Jesus to atone for our sins? Evidently God would prefer to spare us this punishment. If we still reject His offer of forgiveness, what else can He do? If I am drowning, and somebody throws me a life preserver, I can still choose not to grab hold of it, but that would not be the fault of the person who tried to rescue me.

SOMETHING WE CHOOSE FOR OURSELVES

"I protest," the student shouted as he kicked our Christian book table.

"What seems to be the problem?" I asked.

"I protest your teaching. I think it is unfair that I am not going to Heaven simply because I'm not a Christian."

"Friend," I said, "you don't want to go to Heaven."

He stopped short, looking very confused. "What do you mean I don't wanna go to Heaven?"

"I think you have a misconception of what Heaven will be like. Heaven is not some big cloud where angels sit around and strum harps. Heaven is not some island where native women fan you with palm branches and stick grapes in your mouth. Heaven is a place where you will serve and obey God for the rest of eternity. You don't even want to serve and obey Him now. What makes you think you'll want to do it for the rest of eternity? Hell is a place where you'll be all by yourself and nobody will tell you what to do."

I'll never forget his reaction. After a second of pondering he said, "That sounds fair."

DESCRIPTIONS OF HELL

"Granted, those who end up in Hell have chosen to go there, but Hell is not described in the Bible as a mere prison or separation from God. Instead, it is a place where people will be tortured by burning forever."

Actually, we do not need to jump to such a conclusion because the facts are not that certain. It is true that we see an image of fire in many New Testament passages, but we must examine such passages in their cultural context.

> *But anyone who says, "You fool!" will be in danger of the fire of Hell. – Matthew 5:22*

The word Jesus used for *Hell* was *Gehenna*. This referred specifically to the Valley of Hinnom in the southwest part of Jerusalem.[1] Considered a cursed place to the Jews with a history of idol worship, the area was now being used as a public garbage dump where refuse was actually burned. This suggests a different kind of image than what people usually think of concerning Hell. Perhaps the notion of being "discarded as trash" was Jesus' primary point. In using the word *Gehenna,* then, Jesus may simply be saying, "Those who don't serve God, as they were created to do, are going to end up in God's cosmic junk heap." It is not necessarily a location where people burn forever. The fire description may accompany the word *Gehenna* simply because of the association in people's minds between garbage and garbage burning in the Valley of Hinnon. Of course this doesn't take away from the fact that Jesus still views Hell as a real and horrible place to be avoided at all costs.

It is true that elsewhere Jesus talks about an *eternal* fire, but that may just be His way of describing an "everlasting wasteland" using again the language people associated with trash.

Then He will say to those on his left, depart from me, you who are cursed, into the eternal fire prepared for the devil and his angels. (Matthew 25:41)

Interestingly enough, fire is not the only image Jesus associated with Hell. Compare the following verse.

.. and throw the worthless servant outside into the darkness where there will be weeping and gnashing of teeth. – Matthew 25:30

A place of darkness seems to invoke a much different (although no less unpleasant) picture.

"But aren't there passages where Hell is described in greater detail, with fire being a part of that detail?"

Yes, but the more detailed passages come to us through different styles of communication. In Luke 16:19-31, Jesus tells the story of a selfish rich man who would not feed the poor. After he dies, he ends up in Hell while Lazarus, a poor beggar goes to Heaven. The rich man was actually able to look up to Heaven and see Abraham comforting Lazarus. Hell, in this parable is definitely described as a "hot place."

Father Abraham, have pity on me and send Lazarus to dip the top of his finger in water and cool my tongue, because I am in agony in this fire. – Luke 16:24

As the story continues, the rich man asks Abraham for permission to return to Earth temporarily and warn his brothers that they too are headed for Hell if they don't change their selfish ways.

Abraham replied, "They have Moses and the Prophets: let them listen to them." "No father Abraham," He said, "but if someone from the dead goes to them, they will repent." He said to Him, "If they do not listen to Moses and the Prophets, they will not be convinced even if someone rises from the dead." – Luke 16:29-31

As I already mentioned, *Moses and the Prophets* was another way of saying *The Bible or The Scriptures.*

We must remember that Jesus is telling us a story here and not reciting a historical account. Hebrew parables were not intended to teach detailed theology, but instead, to convey one basic truth. Here,

the simple but profound message says: "Hell is a place for people who do not obey the Bible." It would be a mistake to use a passage such as this to teach about the location and weather conditions of Hell. Those who do so are obligated to draw additional conclusions about the afterlife. Do we believe that people in Hell can watch people in Heaven and talk to them? Do we believe that Abraham, as opposed to Jesus, will be pronouncing our sentence? Better to read this as it was intended, a parable with one single theme.

Perhaps the most graphic picture of Hell is found in the Book of Revelation, where we find the expression "Lake of Fire" (Revelation 20:11-15). Revelation is a type of Hebrew writing known as Apocalyptic Literature. Such literature is highly symbolic in nature. We do not read Revelation the way we would read a historical narrative like Acts or a clear letter like Romans. For this reason, we would be wise to consider the possibility that just as John talks about images of beasts, birds, bowls, etc. that the Lake of Fire as well may be a kind of exaggerated picture which he saw in his vision. Still, there is no getting around the fact that Revelation is describing the eternal destiny of people and the Lake of Fire (symbolic as it may be) is a definite reference to Hell.

> **"Even if people don't actually burn, why must sinful people go on living for all of eternity? Wouldn't God be more merciful to just destroy them once and for all?"**

Whether people exist in Hell forever as living conscious beings or whether they are destroyed in Hell once and for all, remains a matter of debate amongst theologians. There seems to be better Scriptural evidence for the former, but we will examine both possibilities.

There is a verse in the New Testament suggesting that condemned souls will cease to exist.

Do not be afraid of those that kill the body but cannot kill the soul. Rather, be afraid of the one who can destroy both soul and body in Hell. – Matthew 10:28

Some take this to mean that Hell is a real place but a place where souls are completely annihilated. This could fit well with the image of burning trash since obviously in the garbage dump Gehenna, individual pieces of trash did not burn forever but were eventually consumed. We have already seen, however, that fire was only one of the images Jesus used for Hell. What's pivotal, of course, is the meaning of the word *destroy*. Is the destruction once and for all, or is it an eternal ongoing destruction? I would be inclined to take this passage at face value and interpret the destruction as final if not for other passages that seem to teach something quite different.

Multitudes who sleep in the dust of the earth shall awake, some to everlasting life, others to shame and everlasting contempt. – Daniel 12:2

This time the key phrase is "everlasting contempt." At first, such words would seem to settle the question left over from Matthew 10:28, but we must be fair. If Daniel suggests that there is more than one way to read Matthew, Matthew likewise suggests that there is more than one way to read Daniel. Here as well, we can ponder two possibilities. Is this a description of one who felt shame during judgment and is now in everlasting contempt by nature of the fact that he has ceased to exist or is this describing a conscious eternal state? The ancient rabbis considered both scenarios and the question remained open.[2] In context, the emphasis seems to be upon the awakening from sleep. *Sleep* in those days was a common phrase for *death*, based upon the Jewish view that death was only temporary, preceding a resurrection. It would seem that Daniel is describing a time when people wake up and remain awake for all of eternity whether in Heaven or in Hell but from this one passage, it is still difficult to draw a final conclusion.

Better detail is found in Revelation 20. Here we see a much more vivid description of the resurrection.

Then I saw a great white throne and Him who was seated on it. Earth and sky fled from his presence, and there was no place for them. And I saw the dead, great and small standing before the throne, and books were opened. Another book was opened which is the book of life. The dead were judged according to what they had done as recorded in the books. The sea gave up the dead that were in it and death and Hades gave up the dead that were in them. Then death and Hades were thrown into the lake of fire. The lake of fire is the second death. If anyone's name was not found written in the book of life, he was thrown into the lake of fire. – Revelation 20:11-15

The phrase "second death" is referring to the fact that people had already died and resurrected. Ironically, some are now going to die again. Hades is a spiritual jail, so to speak, a holding cell where souls await final judgment (1 Peter 3:18-20; Jude 6). The soul is reunited with the body while standing before the throne of Jesus and Jesus throws body and soul together into the Lake of Fire. Earlier we see that Satan is already in this Lake:[3]

And the devil who deceived them was thrown into the lake of burning sulfur, where the beast and the false prophet had been thrown. They will be tormented day and night for ever and ever. – Revelation 20:10

The experience of Hell is clearly described here as a place of continual and conscious torment. Since the accompanying verses show that some people will end up in the same place, we assume that the experience is ongoing for them as well.

I mentioned earlier that Revelation is a book very symbolic in nature. If the "lake" is only an image, one might wonder if the description of everlasting torture is also an exaggerated phrase, but keep in mind that plainer books in the Bible are also talking about Hell. We have already seen Jesus giving straight-forward teaching to His disciples and He described Hell as an eternal place (Matthew 25:41). It makes sense to wonder why it is eternal if it is not going to hold people eternally. Still, we will never understand the metaphysics of Hell in this life, and the Bible does not seem to be going out of its way to explain it.[4] What we know clearly from the Bible is that that some kind of Hell exists and that it is an extremely unhappy place, whatever or wherever it is. God warns people to avoid Hell by turning from their sin and receiving forgiveness.

CHILDREN OF GOD

"It still seems cruel to imagine a Father sending his children to Hell for any reason."

God does not send his children to Hell. Neither is every human being a child of God. We are all creations of God, but we are not all His children. You become a child of God by asking God to adopt you. You are then reborn into His family.

Yet to those who received Him, to those who believed in his name, He gave the right to become children of God. – John 1:12

This doesn't mean that God loves anybody else less. After all, He has given us every opportunity to repent. God is grieved when, despite the opportunities, people still choose to end up in Hell. Still, just for the record, God's children, the ones who allowed Him to rescue them from the "orphanage," the ones He personally raises and trains, will not end up in Hell.

CONCLUSION

In this chapter, we have taken one area of concern and used it to address an equal area of concern. Some may think they are bothered about a God who would send people to Hell, but they are also bothered about the evil in the world and they would be quite upset to think of a God who did not care about the sufferings of the very beings He created. We conclude that a just and loving God would hold people accountable and keep evil out of His paradise kingdom. Although the Bible does not give a lot of detail, it describes Hell as a real location and ultimate destiny of those who rebel against God.

Of course no discussion of Hell would be complete without an examination of God's merciful alternative, the forgiveness of Jesus Christ. Appropriately, this will be the subject of our next chapter.

---

1 In this valley, King Ahaz had once promoted the worship of Molech. Children were burned as a sacrifice to this God (II Chronicles 28:3). Later, a better king named Josiah decreed that this valley would be a cursed place.

"He desecrated Topheth which was in the Valley of Ben Hinnom, so no one could use it to sacrifice his son or daughter in the fire to Molech" (II Kings 23:10).

2 The two ancient and opposing Jewish schools of thought, Shammai and Hillel came to different conclusions about Hell. Shammai did read Daniel 12:2 to mean eternal, conscious punishment. The liberal School of Hillel, on the other hand, believed that Gehenna would someday cease and that its inhabitants would be annihilated since they were not worthy of Gan Eden (a term for the paradise afterlife). Exceptionally wicked people will continue to exist somewhere, but the fires of Gehenna will still cease (R.H. 16b *Babylonian Talmud*).

3 Space does not permit a detailed discussion of Satan but a few comments are warranted. Even many who believe in God have a much harder time accepting the reality of the devil. I submit that this doubt emanates from the false and mythical images that come to mind when the subject of Satan arises. Satan is not presented in the Bible as a red hot creature with horns and a pitchfork. He is instead some kind of intelligent alien being, a creation of God, spiritual in essence, who existed in Heaven with a certain measure of authority designated from God and who later rebelled against God because of his pride (1 Timothy 3:7). As part of his rebellion, he works in the world to deceive people and lead them away from Jesus (Matthew 13:19) but, as indicated in Revelation 20:10, he himself will be punished in Hell and will not be in charge of Hell. The popular idea of Satan ruling Hell is found in Milton's Paradise Lost, not the Bible. For a fuller discussion of Satan, see Hal Lindsey, *Satan Is Alive and Well and Living on Planet Earth.*

4 The Jewish Talmud does contain descriptions about the location and nature of Hell. But these were speculative opinions of Rabbis who differed with each other. One description places Hell under the earth, (*Taan.* 10a, *Babylonian Talmud*), another, above the firmament and still another, behind some mysterious mountains of darkness somewhere west of the world (*Tamid* 23b, *Babylonian Talmud*). To this author, it makes sense to think of Heaven and Hell as a part of some other, unseen dimension.

103

Chapter 6

IS JESUS REALLY THE ONLY WAY TO GOD?

"Isn't there a difference between believing in a God who sends evil people to Hell and a God who condemns us simply because we don't believe in Jesus? Isn't this an awfully closed-minded idea?"

At the beginning of any kind of inquiry we should certainly be open to a wide range of possibilities, but sooner or later, everybody closes their minds. We remain open only for a while with the objective of finding what we are looking for, learning new facts, and *eventually closing our minds*. Whether or not the world rotates around the sun may have been an open question centuries ago, but scientists have long since drawn their conclusions.

A student at UC Santa Barbara once accused me of being closed-minded and insisted that if I had an open mind I could not possibly believe that there is only one way to God.

"Let me ask you a question," I said. "Are you open-minded enough to consider the *possibility* that there is only one way to God?"

"What?"

"You say you have an open mind. All right then, are you open-minded enough to at least ponder the possibility that Jesus may be the only way?"

"Absolutely not!"

"Really? This is interesting. You can't even consider it?" "Never."

"Why can't you?"

"Because such a belief is closed-minded."

"But the consideration of the belief isn't. An open mind says, 'Maybe there are a thousand ways to God. Maybe there are two ways to God. Maybe there are no ways to God. Maybe there is only one way to God.' That is a truly open mind."

"O.K., I suppose people should be open enough to consider Jesus. But it is still hard to imagine that Jesus would equate allegiance to Himself with the only road into God's Kingdom. In fact, let me ask. Did Jesus really offer Himself as the only escape from Hell? I have heard it taught that He never really made such claims and that this idea was developed years later by the Church."

This is a pertinent question because often people express great respect for Jesus while denying that He ever commanded His followers to go out and preach the Gospel. A student at Mesa Community College in Arizona drove this point home to me once on a sunny afternoon.

"I think this business of Jesus being the only way to God is the most lame-brain, pin-headed, narrow – minded thing I ever heard."

Instead of arguing, I politely asked the opinionated student for his appraisal of Jesus Himself.

"Jesus Himself? Oh…no problem there. I think He was a wonderful teacher, a good philosopher and a great humanitarian."

"I see. Do you know where the idea of Jesus being the 'only way' came from?" "No, I imagine the teaching was developed by churches over the years."
"Not really. This idea came from Jesus."

The student was flabbergasted. He had just labeled a "wonderful teacher, philosopher and humanitarian" as a "pin-head."

I would consider it a waste of time to defend a mere Church tradition. Remember, a Christian by definition, is one who follows Christ. There is no point in explaining the narrow nature of Christianity if such teaching were foreign to the founder of our faith. Our need for salvation was the very purpose of Jesus' mission.

I tell you the truth, unless a man is born again, He cannot see the kingdom of God. – John 3:3

Mysterious words? Yes indeed. But their context will shed some light. Whatever being born again means, it is somehow related to entering God's Kingdom. In Mark 10, Jesus equates the entry to God's Kingdom with the reception of *eternal life*. We do not need to look far into the gospels to discover the qualification for eternal life.

Whoever believes in the Son has eternal life, but whoever rejects the Son will not see life, for God's wrath remains on Him. – John 3:36

These words came from John the Baptist. John's message and ministry had already been publicly condoned by Jesus. Jesus Himself gave a similar statement in John 3:18.

"Whoever believes in Him is not condemned, but whoever does not believe stands condemned already because He has not believed in the name of God's one and only Son."

Consider as well, John 14:6:

"I am the way and the truth and the life. No one comes to the Father except through me."

Is Jesus talking about one of many paths to God? Is He acknowledging that each person's religion is "beautiful in its own way?" Hardly. The words do not read, "I am *a* truth," or "I am *a* way."

With what authority did Jesus speak so boldly? Even His own disciples wanted to know.

Philip said,

"Lord, show us the Father and that will be enough for us."

Jesus answered,

"Don't you know me, Philip, even after I have been among you such a long time? Anyone who has seen me has seen the Father. How can you say, 'Show us the Father?' Don't you believe that I am in the Father and the Father is in me?"-John 14:8-10

Imagine following somebody for years because He seems to have such a special insight into spiritual matters. Now, at a quiet private moment toward the end of His ministry, Jesus lets His disciples in on a little secret. The reason He knows so much about God is that He *is* God. Can't you just feel the shivers that must have accompanied this incredible conversation?

Whatever form and power God the Son had in eternity past, He gave it all up and somehow transformed Himself into a real human being (Philippians 2:5-8). He knew hunger, thirst, pain and suppressive government rule. Although He never sinned, He was tempted (Hebrews 2:18) and the experience gave Him a special empathy (Hebrews 4:15). It is as though God were saying, "I will not ask you to go through anything which I am unwilling to go through myself." After rising from the dead, Jesus returned to Heaven to rule with the Father, but, although He regained the position of God, He remains in the form of a man for all of eternity, a glorified immortal man certainly, but still a man (Philippians 2:9-11, 1 John 3:2).

It is true that Jesus is one member of a co-equal Trinity, but this mystery does not dilute His divine identity. The other two members retained their position while Jesus walked the earth.[1] He lived in obedience to the Father (John 15:10) and He performed miracles by the power of the Holy Spirit (Matthew 12:22-28).

Now then, what is so illogical about God Himself saying, "Hi, I'm God and I, God, am the only way to God?"

"OK. If Jesus was God, He had the right to say whatever He

wanted. But why is He so concerned about mere beliefs?"

The word *believe* in Greek (pisteuo) did not mean mere intellectual assent but rather obedience. One is saved by making a decision to *obey* Jesus.[2] It is true that we need His forgiveness and it is also true that without the power of the Holy Spirit we would be incapable of following God, but God is not going to give a theology exam on judgment day. He is instead concerned about people turning from their sins.

A student at UC Santa Barbara once approached my Christian book table with a sly grin. "You know," he said, "I like to get high on a joint every once in a while, but I would never dream of setting up a table with a sign, telling people that they had to get high on joints too." In other words, where did I get the nerve to say that what works for me (Jesus), must work for him as well or else?

I said to him, "If Jesus were merely some radical mind trip, I would see your point, but let me ask you something. If you knew the cure for cancer, would you share it with people?"

After a bit of hesitation, he answered, "Of course."

"Would you agree that when we do discover the cure of cancer, that there will be only one cure?"

"I suppose."

"And on that day, when somebody claims to have this exclusive cure, could we not accuse the person of being closed-minded? After all, doesn't it take a lot of nerve to call just one treatment the cure for cancer? Maybe penicillin is the cure. Maybe Vitamin C is the cure."

Jesus is the cure for a disease far more deadly than cancer. This disease is sin.

"But is sin really our fault? I can accept the definition of sin as selfishness, and I can understand why God wouldn't want us

109

to live selfishly, but isn't it also true that the Bible talks about a sin nature? Isn't this something we are born with? Isn't this something we can't control? If so, how then can a loving God condemn us?"

It is true that people are born with a sin nature. As mentioned in Chapter 3, human beings do not follow their consciences nearly as much as they should. Although we can change our actions, we cannot change our thoughts and motives. I may hate feeling jealous or bitter or angry or lustful, but there is no button on my side that I can push to make those feelings go away. I may have good feelings as well, but if I am half clean and half dirty, I still need a shower.

Paul did an excellent job of describing this condition.

We know that the law is spiritual: but I am unspiritual, sold as a slave to sin. I do not understand what I do. For what I want to do I do not do, but what I hate I do. And if I do what I do not want to do, I agree that the law is good. As it is, it is no longer I myself who do it, but it is sin living in me. I know that nothing good lives in me, that is, in my sinful nature. For I have the desire to do what is good, but I cannot carry it out. For what I do is not the good I want to do, but the evil I do not want to do, this I do...it is no longer I who do it, but it is sin living in me that does it. – Romans 7:14-20

What exactly is this sin nature? Is it some kind of curse or whammy God physically puts on babies at birth? No. *Our sin nature is our separation from God.* People are composed of body, soul, and spirit. The soul is yourself, your will and your personality. The spirit is a part of your soul, that part which is in tune with God and His morals through the conscience (Hebrews 4:12; Romans 7:22). The very first human beings were created sinless, but with an ability to choose right from wrong. For all intents and purposes, they were born into fellowship with God. Another way to say it is that they were "plugged into God." They were spiritually connected with Him. When they later turned from Him in disobedience, God unplugged Himself from people and from the world (Romans 8:20-21).

You will recall that God warned Adam and Eve that they would die on the day they ate the forbidden fruit (Genesis 2:16-17). You will also recall that they did not actually die, at least not physically. But all kinds of sudden internal changes took place as Adam and Eve experienced a shame they had never felt before (Genesis 3:10). What happened, of course, is that they died spiritually; more specifically, their spirits died while their souls and bodies remained alive. As children of Adam and Eve, we are all born "unplugged" that is, our spirits exist but in a "dead" or "malfunctioning" way. Although we still have a sense of God (the conscience), the separation keeps us from submitting completely to the influence of His Spirit. As a result, men and women run their own lives, something God never intended for them to do. Consequently, we develop many sinful habits. That, along with the absence of God within, is what the Bible means by a sin nature.

"But if I really inherited this nature from Adam, then God should not blame me. This wasn't my fault. Why should I pay for what some idiot did years ago? Who knows, if I had been there in the garden, I might not have eaten the forbidden fruit."

First, of all, Christ is the only one who paid for the "idiot" and, as a result, you need never pay. It is true that you and I were born with a sin nature, but it is not true that we would have acted contrary to Adam, had the world only been fortunate enough to have one of us as the first human being. Adam acted on behalf of people as a species, doing what God knew any of us would have done. If it hadn't been him, it would have been me (Romans 5:12).

"Oh, come on. That's a very convenient thing to say. But I guess we'll never know, will we?"

Yes we will. God has proven the point by giving us His law.

The law was added so that the trespass might increase. – Romans 5:20

Although my sin nature contains thoughts and feelings I cannot change apart from a supernatural working of God's Spirit, I am, nevertheless, painfully aware of many occasions, where, without being compelled, I sinned anyway. This has even been true in my Christian life in spite of the Holy Spirit who can teach me to turn away from sin if I will only let Him (I Corinthians 10:13). Adam's trespass has been repeated time and time again. Therefore, although people are sinners by nature (thanks to Adam), they are also sinners by choice (thanks to themselves). Certainly things are now rearranged. Adam was surrounded by good and he had one path to evil, the tree of the knowledge of good and evil. Today, we are surrounded by evil, a "negative Garden of Eden" with one path back to God, Jesus Christ. What is the difference between being with God and leaving Him or being away from God and refusing to meet Him?

So then, I am responsible for the sins I choose to commit, but I am not responsible for having been born with a sin nature. That, I did not deserve. But neither did I deserve to be completely free from all sin (inward and outward) as a result of Jesus' death on the cross. This too is undeserved. As you can see, things even out.

> *Consequently, just as the result of one trespass was condemnation for all men, so also the result of one act of righteousness was justification that brings life for all men. For just as through the disobedience of the one man the many were made sinners, so also through the obedience of the one man, the many will be made righteous. – Romans 5:18-19*

Many years ago the famous evangelist Billy Graham was a guest on the Donahue show. In a tongue and cheek fashion, Donahue expressed displeasure over the Christian doctrine of an inherited sin nature and said something to the effect of, "I am unhappy about the way I was born. What can I do about that?"

"What you can do," said Graham, "is become born again."

A loving God does not want to send anybody to Hell. This is the very reason Jesus came. Imagine God saying to Himself, "I love Sandra very much, but Sandra has sinned. I cannot let her into my kingdom, for that would make my kingdom wicked. No, the sin has to be paid for."

Being without limitations, God already had a plan: "Supposing I were to justly judge Sandra by completely destroying her? And then, supposing I were to create a brand new Sandra who is perfect, spotless and sinless? Supposing Sandra were spared the pain and torment of the experience, being conscious only of the positive transition?"

This proposed solution to the paradox was literally fulfilled by the crucifixion of Jesus Christ. The cross is the climax of God's love and justice combined. Although physically you did not hang on that cross, God (in a manner that we do not understand), looked at Jesus as if He were you! In some mysterious way, Jesus was actually judged for your sin!

> *He Himself bore our sins in his body on the tree so that we might die to sins and live to righteousness: by his wounds, you have been healed. – 1 Peter 2:24*

"Born again" literally refers to our future on judgment day when we will be raised from the dead and recreated, body, soul, and spirit.

> *Therefore, if anyone is in Christ, he is a new creation. The old has gone, the new has come. – 2 Corinthians 5:17*

> *If we have been united with Him in his death, we will certainly also be united with Him in his resurrection. – Romans 6:5*

Although this reality exists in our future, it is the present to God since He exists outside of time (2 Peter 3:8). Therefore, God tells us to become born again now, and in so doing, view ourselves the way He views us. As a "down payment" for our future inheritance, God does two things: First, He gives us a resurrected spirit promising to transform the rest of us when we meet Jesus in Heaven. Second, He personally resides in our souls with His Holy Spirit. The fellowship of our new spirit and the Holy Spirit together give us a subjective sense that God has adopted us and we actually begin to think of Him as a personal Father.

For you did not receive a spirit that makes you a slave again to fear, but you received the Spirit of sonship. And by Him we cry "Abba Father." The Spirit Himself testifies with our spirit that we are God's children. Now if we are children, then we are heirs, heirs of God and co-heirs with Christ. – Romans 8:15-17

How much more should we submit to the Father of our spirits and live? – Hebrews 12:9

Having believed, you were marked in Him with a seal, the promised Holy Spirit, who is a deposit guaranteeing our inheritance until the redemption of those who are God's possession. – Ephesians 1:13-14

"But people must still choose this relationship and according to the Bible many won't, which means that although God doesn't want to, He will still send multitudes to Hell. Why then, did God give us a free will if He knew we would misuse it? Doesn't this make God responsible for the evil in the world along with the evil that will someday inhabit Hell?"

Evidently, being in God's image is considered an ideal quality characterized by certain freedom. The alternative is to be a programmed robot or a mindless animal. You may question your free will, but you will have a hard time convincing me that you aren't grateful for it. Without this quality, you would not possess the unique personality and creativity that makes you a special individual. How many wars and revolutions have been fought in the name of freedom? Doesn't this say something about how people truly cherish their free will?

Just as God knew that men and women would misuse their free wills, He also knew ahead of time that Christ would die for our sins (Ephesians 1:4-5). This projected forgiveness gave God the leeway to teach us through our own stupid mistakes as we learn to appreciate righteousness and use our free will properly.

I never appreciate good health until I get sick. In a similar manner, humans as a species acted like the prodigal son, who insisted on leaving the security and protection of his Father, to make his own life in the world (Luke 15:11-31). We have seen the horrifying results of human life separated from God.

Now, having experienced evil, we look toward a future day when paradise is restored. We have learned to appreciate goodness. This is not to say that evil was necessary or preferable. I am merely describing the manner in which God taught us not to misuse our freedom by providing a vision of its ugly effects.

The story of Adam and Eve is frequently referred to as a fairy tale. I used to view it that way myself until a careful study of the "story" brought about an interesting discovery. Genesis 1-3 is the most logical explanation I have ever seen to account for our world's condition. Earlier I described life as a paradise invaded. Genesis offers a reason for this picture. Ignore the Genesis account if you wish, but you will only have to search for a similar explanation. The world was once a wonderful place but people did not appreciate their paradise. They wanted to know what evil was.

"Where is God," I always hear, "when wars and crimes kill people? Where is God when children starve to death?"

I have a better question. Where are people? The principles of love, kindness and sharing originated from God. These are His commands. Suffering in the world does not convince me that God doesn't exist. Instead, it convinces me that God knew what He was talking about when He commanded us to feed the poor and when He said, "Thou shalt not kill." The devastating results of evil display crystal clear evidence that we should have obeyed God all along. God was being loving when He established guidelines and limitations.

"But wouldn't these guidelines and limitations violate the very free will God supposedly wants us to have?"

Limitations do not obliterate our will. They exist as a choice for the person who wants to live righteously. As mentioned in Chapter 4, God is primarily concerned with how we treat people. He is not out to stifle

115

our creativity or to nullify our unique personalities.

"Why should the limitations be introduced on judgment day? Why doesn't God just destroy all evil now?"

Who would be left? In God's eyes, you too are evil. Should He do a thorough job by wiping you out? Evil has its varying manifestations, but no one person is completely free of evil. If we want God to be merciful with us, we must live with the fact that He will offer His grace to everybody. Rest assured, God will deal drastically and adequately with all evil. The person who does not accept Christ will pay the penalty for his/her own sin. There can never be a more final, deadly judgment of evil than total, ultimate, separation from the joys of life and the presence of God. When we remember that humans, with their free wills, are graciously granted an entire lifetime to either accept or reject Jesus, we can understand that for a designated period of time, evil must be allowed. Since not everybody will accept His grace and since evil still must be dealt with, we are left with an affirmation of Hell.

CONCLUSION

Our purpose in this chapter was to explain the relationship between God's justice and mercy. Although God delights in creatures of free will, such freedom has certain responsibilities. The violation of these responsibilities results in sin. Humans are sinners by nature and by choice. Through Jesus, and His sacrifice, all sin can be done away with. This was the teaching of His Gospel. The authority of the message comes from the fantastic truth that Jesus was actually God in the form of a man. These claims, incredible as they are, will be considered by anyone with a truly open mind.

---

1 Do not waste your time trying to figure out how God could exist in multiple places, all the while maintaining oneness. At the moment, God has chosen not to scientifically explain His essence. If we could figure out everything about God, He wouldn't be much of a God. We must simply trust that He has revealed all we need to know (Deuteronomy. 29:29).

2 For a fuller discussion from this author on the relationship between obedience to Christ and the equal biblical truth that our salvation is all by grace, see *A Call to Radical Discipleship (Mission to the Americas*, Wheaton, Illinois, 1997) p. 11-41.

Chapter 7

How Will God Judge the People Who Never Heard of Jesus?

"If Jesus is the only way to God, how does God judge the people who never heard of Christ? Countless cultures have survived generation after generation apart from any missionary activity. They never met a preacher and they never read a Bible. Is God going to send all of these poor, ignorant people to Hell?"

At first glance, we would seem to have a difficult problem in connection with the saviorhood of Jesus. The Word of God does not address this issue directly. Although the New Testament provides many clear details about those who *have* heard the Gospel, it has little to say about people who die without exposure to the message. We do have some clues which may shed light on the subject. Such clues suggest that in certain cases a loving God will take a person's ignorance into consideration, but before even going there, let us lay out some important theological backgrounds.

A COMMON HERITAGE

We must first of all remember that geography does not erase sin. This human condition is the same wherever people live. God would be no less just if He pushed our entire planet into the sun without forgiving anybody. He owes us absolutely nothing. I suspect that when most people inquire about "those who never heard" they are referring to the "innocent man who lives a good life even though he hasn't been exposed to Christianity." Until we realize that no such person exists, the question of "ignorance" cannot be adequately discussed.

If you asked most people to name the greatest humanitarian of the twentieth century, undoubtedly the name of India's former spiritual leader and pacifist revolutionary, Mahatma Gandhi would surface. Since Gandhi was not a Christian, he is frequently offered as an example of a great man whom God could not possibly reject. One couldn't find a better example of a person with true integrity who lived an exceedingly virtuous life. Interestingly enough, this appraisal was not shared by Gandhi Himself. Gandhi considered his heart to be quite sinful. What made him different is that his sin did

concern him a lot, and Ghandi struggled so much to improve himself that by contrast to those around him he came across as a very good man.[1]

> *What shall we conclude then? Are we any better? Not at all. We have already made the charge that Jews and Gentiles are all under sin. As it is written, 'There is none righteous, not even one… All have turned away, they have together become worthless.' – Romans 3:9,12*

With this in mind, we can examine a more genuine problem: Assuming that God in His love and mercy died for all sinners, how will He offer this undeserved grace to the individual who has not met a missionary?

SEEKING

I submit that no one is beyond the range of God's communication. In Chapter 3, I suggested the possibility of God speaking only to those who desire such revelation. What makes sense to a philosopher is a fact for the theologian. Our Bible makes it abundantly clear that those who seek God, find God.

> *You will seek me and you will find me when you seek with all your heart. – Jeremiah 29:13*

> *God did this so that men would seek Him and perhaps reach out for Him and find Him, though He is not far from each one of us. – Acts 17:27*

> *Ask and it will be given to you, seek and you will find, knock and the door will be opened to you. For everyone who asks receives; he who seeks finds and to him who knocks the door will be opened.*

118

Which of you fathers, if your son asks for a fish will give him a snake instead, or if he asks for an egg will give him a scorpion? If you then, though you are evil, know how to give good gifts to your children, how much more will your Father in Heaven give the Holy Spirit to those who ask Him. – Luke 11:9-11

...anyone who comes to Him must believe that He exists and that He rewards those who earnestly seek Him. – Hebrews 11:6

Actually, the term *seek* is only a description of our conscious experience. Simultaneous to our "search" is a working from God's Spirit of which we are unaware. Apart from the "whisper" or "suggestion" of the Spirit, sinful people would never look for God.

There is no one who understands, no one who seeks God. – Romans 3:11

This is why I told you that no one can come to me unless the Father has enabled Him. – John 6:65

If humans do not seek God on their own initiative, perhaps we would do better to use the word *respond*. To solve our puzzle, we must therefore ask about the nature of man's response. As a key to unlocking this door, I will return to our study of the conscience. Through the conscience, God can communicate with people directly.

Indeed when Gentiles who do not have the law do by nature things required by the law, they are a law for themselves, even though they do not have the law, since they show that the requirements of the law are written on their hearts, their consciences also bearing witness and their thoughts now accusing, now even defending them. – Romans 2:14-15

There is a close relationship between the probing Spirit of God and man's inner witness to morality. In John 16 the Holy Spirit's task is described as a work similar to that of our conscience.

When He comes, He will convict the world of guilt in regard to sin and righteousness and judgment. – John 16:8

119

Think of the conscience as a kind of radar, homing in on the Spirit of God. A positive reaction to this divinely implanted radar is really a response to the small degree of light God has stored within each of us. If a person follows the initial "spark," God will provide fuller and deeper revelation. The more we respond, the more God works. Ultimately, this light will lead to a direct understanding of Jesus Christ. One can resist this illumination any time along the way. In a final analysis, the choice to permanently ignore the conscience is no different than a decision to forever disobey God. As you can see, it is possible to reject Jesus Christ without even knowing what you are rejecting. *God is not concerned so much about the understanding of doctrine as He is concerned about our quest for morality.*

Blessed are those who hunger and thirst for righteousness, for they will be filled. – Matthew 5:8

Jesus is the only means to quenching such a thirst. The woman who desires a righteous life will somehow find Christ, regardless of her knowledge or background. If this person is honestly attempting to live free of guilt, she is destined for some painful frustration. She will soon discover a continual condemnation. This depression will lead to an introspection of life. The woman will look for God without realizing it. She may call it a search for truth, purpose, peace or righteousness, but what is really going on? The spiritual element within is crying for mercy, longing to be plugged into the source of love.

Most people ignore their inner guilt. With frequent rationalization, they slowly submerge the conscience, making it dim, weak and ineffective.

A rejection of Jesus can happen at the late stage of hearing the Gospel message or the early stage of spiritual sensitivity. The result is the same. Both individuals are refusing to live as they were intended. In other words, those who never encounter Christ would never have wanted to encounter Christ.

This is the verdict. Light has come into the world, but men loved darkness instead of light because their deeds were evil. – John 3:19

SOME BIBLICAL PROFILES

There are two cases in the New Testament where we see God communicating to seeking individuals apart from missionary activity.

Acts 10 gives the dramatic account of a Roman centurion named Cornelius. Cornelius was familiar only with Judaism. He knew nothing of Christianity. One night, while praying to God, an angel appeared to Cornelius.

> *The angel answered, "Your prayers and gifts to the poor have come up as a remembrance before God. Now, send men to Joppa to bring back a man named Simon, who is called Peter." – Acts 10:4-6*

Judaism was an old covenant, rendered inoperative by God. But Judaism was all Cornelius knew. Here we see the graciousness of our Lord as He overlooks a man's outdated theology and instead honors his seeking heart. Had it not been for this timely vision, Cornelius would never have met Peter, the man who later shared Christ. We should also note that even the centurion's frustrated attempt to "live a good life" (giving to the poor) was viewed as a search for the Creator of goodness.

Another significant example is the conversion of the Apostle Paul (also called Saul). On the road to Damascus, Paul actually heard the audible voice of Christ Himself. Were it not for this divine encounter, Paul would have continued with his intellectual certainty that Christians were heretics.

Was Paul's conversion a special favor of God, granted out of the clear blue sky, or was it somehow related to a disturbed conscience? To answer this question, we must study Paul's own testimony.

> *We all fell to the ground and I heard a voice saying to me in Aramaic, "Saul, Saul, why do you persecute me? It is hard for you to kick against the goads." – Acts 26:14*

The word *goad* referred to a bar of wooden spikes attached to a wagon. The purpose of this contraption was to prevent the oxen from kicking. It was quite self-defeating for an ox to slam his foot into sharp spokes. Of course, the harder he kicked, the stronger the pain. So it was with Rabbi Saul, a member of that unique Jewish court called the Sanhedrin. Under the mistaken impression that he was doing God a favor, Saul persecuted Christians to the point of beating some and voting for the death of others. But a haunting suspicion of "being in the wrong" tormented the zealous arbitrator with a self – inflicted agony likened very much to "kicking against the goads." Paul's zeal for God, bridled and redirected by the conscience, eventually led him to that climactic moment on the Damascus road. In a manner unrecognized by the early church, Paul was looking for Jesus in spite of his ignorance.

Even though I was once a blasphemer and persecutor and a violent man, I was shown mercy because I acted in ignorance and unbelief. – 1 Timothy 1:13

The appearance of an angel or an audible voice from the sky are only two examples of God's unique communication. When a man is searching for his master, Jesus will move mountains to make Himself known. Perhaps He will speak through visions or dreams. Perhaps He will send a missionary. The possibilities are endless. We can rest assured that a just and loving God will feed every hungry soul.

THE SAME SEARCH IN MODERN TIMES

Her name was Rennie. She was sitting on the lawn at UCSB, looking rather pensive, when I approached her with a religious questionnaire. Rennie found my sudden appearance to be most coincidental. Recently she had been asking herself questions such as "What is the meaning of life? Why am I here? What is my purpose? What is truth?" Not only did she ponder those subjects but she had actually been praying to God for answers moments before I arrived! We talked for quite some time before Rennie finally expressed an interest in praying with me to receive the Spirit of Christ. Her prayer contained the most heartbreaking words I had ever heard. "God, you know how long I have been searching for You. Just today, sitting here on the grass

I asked you to reveal yourself and within moments you…" Rennie stopped short, unable to control her tears. "Thank you God," she finally choked out.

OTHER PROBLEMS

"If God is really making Himself known, why do we have so many places where Christianity is not found?"

Primarily God would prefer to reach people through the Church. The Church has not often done its job in obeying the Great Commission (Matthew 28:19-20).

Unfortunately, there is also another reason: Very few people grieve over their sin. As a result, they are not looking for God. It should not surprise us that Christianity is scarce. As a matter of fact, Jesus predicted this very thing.

> *Enter through the narrow gate. For wide is the gate and broad is the road that leads to destruction and many enter through it. But small is the gate and narrow is the road that leads to life and only a few find it. – Matthew 7:13-14*

IGNORANCE

"What about the people who lived before Jesus came?"

The Old Testament is filled with saints who did not understand the Gospel. These people did understand the need to repent of all sin and obey the living God. They also understood the corrupt nature which prevented them from adequately fulfilling this task. Finally, they comprehended God's mercy and forgiveness. These patriarchs and Israelites knew that blood atonement for sin was required as part of the Mosaic law (Leviticus). But they knew nothing of a man named Jesus Christ who would die for their trespasses in 33 A.D. as the ultimate sacrifice. Nevertheless, when Jesus died, He paid for the sins of Abraham, Moses, David and any other Hebrew who sought after his Lord. These Israelites did not enter Heaven apart from their Messiah.

There has never been more than one way to save a soul, not even under the Old Covenant. It's just that certain individuals wore darker glasses as they latched onto the redeeming blood of the cross. Their animal sacrifices enabled them to see a picture similar to what Jesus would eventually do.

"But there were many who lived before Jesus, not just the people of Israel."

Yes there were. This is why Paul describes a similar understanding with ignorant Gentiles in his sermon on Mars Hill.

"Men of Athens! I see that in every way you are very religious. For as I walked around and observed your objects of worship, I even found an altar with this inscription on it, TO AN UNKNOWN GOD. Now, what you worship as something unknown, I am going to proclaim to you...In the past, God overlooked such ignorance but now He commands all people everywhere to repent." – Acts 17:22-23,30

I do not take this to mean that the ignorance of every person is an automatic ticket into Heaven. I believe Paul was thinking of repentant Greeks who grieved over their sin, people who would have accepted Jesus had they been given the opportunity.

"Could people today have their ignorance overlooked in a similar manner? Could they 'latch on to the redeeming blood of the cross with darker glasses?'"

Here we are entering into speculation. We know that God reveals Himself, but we do not know the extent of this revelation in every case. One thing is certain; we can never ascribe to the poisonous teaching that all religions offer a road to God. Nobody will ever enter God's Kingdom apart from Jesus Christ. On the other hand, when Paul gave that speech in Athens, Christianity was already some 20 years old and missionaries had been proclaiming the New Covenant for quite some time. Still, the citizens of Athens had not yet heard the good news. While listening to Paul and hearing his promise that the times of ignorance were being overlooked, a citizen could say to himself, "Yesterday, I had an excuse not to follow Jesus, but now Jesus has made Himself known." This is an important method of biblical interpretation; asking ourselves, "What did this passage mean to the original audience for whom it was prepared?" And to the people of Athens, Paul's speech taught that we are accountable for what we know, not what we don't know. Elsewhere in Scripture Jesus says:

> *"From everyone who has been given much, much will be demanded, and from the one who has been entrusted with much, much more will be asked." – Luke 12:48*

With this in mind, consider the following possibility: We have already seen that a response to the conscience is really a response to the Holy Spirit. The resulting guilt, along with man's intuitive sense of accountability may cause Him to cry out for mercy. Such a person is calling upon the true God, whoever this God may be. He is longing for his wicked heart to be transformed. The one who reaches this point has done all that he can. Jesus Christ promised to accept any repentant individual who begs for God's forgiveness (Luke 18:13). *In short, I believe God will judge people according to what they would have done if they had heard.* I believe He will use their consciences to demonstrate what they would or would not have done. This seems to be the meaning behind Paul's interesting discussion in Romans. We looked earlier at the passage. Recall that Paul is talking here about people who never heard the Gospel and how God will still judge them according to the precepts of their own conscience.

> *...since they show that the requirements of the law are written on their hearts, their consciences also bearing witness and their thoughts now accusing, now even defending them. This will take place on the day when God will judge men's secrets through Jesus Christ as my Gospel declares. – Romans 2:15-16*

Imagine then, two souls standing before God. God turns to the first one and says, "I realize that you never heard the Gospel while living on Earth, but you paid attention to your conscience. You tried to obey it. When you found that you couldn't change the thoughts and motives

125

that your own inner witness condemned, you were frustrated. You wished often that something could be done to make you a better person and you asked help of whatever God was out there. It is obvious to me that you are one who would have responded positively to the Gospel had it come your way."

Then God turns to the second soul. "You didn't hear the Gospel either, but frankly, it wouldn't have made much difference. You ignored your conscience and justified your sin. You rationalized by telling yourself that you were no worse than anyone else, and at times you lied to yourself about right and wrong just to avoid feeling guilty. Had you heard the Gospel, you would have been one of the many who rejected it. This is very obvious. Since you ignored your very own conscience, you certainly would have ignored a message which, among other things, promises my Spirit will reside within and amplify your conscience."

ENTIRE CULTURES LOOKING FOR GOD TOGETHER

There is abundant documentation of remote cultures who sought to serve the one true God, and celebrated the arrival of missionaries as fulfillments of their expectations.

Alonzo Bunker, a late nineteenth century writer, studied a Burmese hill people called the Karen for thirty years and lived amongst them. He reported their belief in one supreme God and their eager, centuries old prediction that a brother would someday visit from far away bringing with him a lost

book written by Ya'wa. Such a book would provide both freedom and instruction on how to better worship Ya'wa.[2]

Karen hymns describe Ya'wa as creator of the entire world. He is also all powerful and all knowing. The Karen even have a story about how people fell away from God:

> Ya'wa formed the world originally.
> He appointed food and drink.

126

He appointed the "fruit of trial."
He caused them to eat the fruit of the tree of trial.
They obeyed not: they believed not Ya'wa...
When they ate the fruit of trial, they became subject to sickness, aging and death.[3]

The parallel to Genesis is so obvious that it barely needs mentioning. The similarity between the Hebrew name for God, Yahweh, and Ya'wa is also noteworthy. But there is no record of any Christian witness to the Karen prior to 1795 when they were first discovered or in the subsequent century which saw only a handful of visitors.[4] We seem to have a fantastic example of people learning scattered truths about God apart from missionary intervention.

The Karen are not the only tribe from that corner of the world with monotheistic views and anticipations of a lost book. Don Richardson documents similar beliefs from the Kachin, Lahu, Shan, Palaung, Naga, Lisa, Wa and Kui.[5] Of the latter he says;

> MacLeish states that Kui tribesmen, living along the Thai-Burma border, actually built houses of worship dedicated to the true God in anticipation of the time when a messenger from God would enter such places of worship with the lost book in his hand to teach the people! No idols were ever placed in such places of worship, but Kui folk would "gather and, in dim uncertain fashion, worship the great God above."[6]

One couldn't ask for better evidence that humans are only so ignorant and that much can be learned about God apart from missionary activity.

OTHER KINDS OF IGNORANCE

"O.K., so maybe God does take ignorance into account for people who live in far off lands or for people who lived before Jesus came. But even here in America many who have heard the Gospel are simply not convinced that it is true. If we die and discover we were wrong, won't God be obligated to judge

127

us as legitimately ignorant people who were merely being honest about what they believed and what they didn't believe?"

I am never bothered by the honest skeptic who isn't convinced of Jesus' claims. Instead, I simply ask about what would happen in the event that God were to make Himself known.

"Then, would you serve Him?" I ask.

The usual words, "Oh yes, certainly," are quickly tested as I begin to suggest ways in which God can be found (i.e., Bible study, historical research, prayer, meditation, immersion into Christian fellowship, etc.).

"Well, I'm not sure I have the time to do those things. With school and work, my schedule is very limited."

Convenient as such an excuse seems to be, that person will still be held accountable. Deep inside, a semi-conscious train of thought is moving on. "Once I discover that Jesus is real, I'll have no excuse to refuse serving Him. But if I leave the door closed, I'll never know for sure what's on the other side. I can live the way I choose. Whenever my conscience bothers me, I may comfort myself in the knowledge that maybe Jesus does not exist after all."

We can easily fool ourselves but God is not tricked by these flake-out maneuvers. The day of judgment will spotlight all hidden motives.

"What about those who die as infants? Obviously an infant cannot choose to repent. In what manner will God handle such a situation?"

Putting aside the blatantly obvious observation that sending a baby to Hell does not seem to be the action of a loving God, many Christians believe there is such a thing as the "age of accountability." That actual term is not found in the Scriptures, but Matthew 12 contains a description of the only sin for which Jesus did not die. This sin is a conscious and final refusal to serve Christ. Since Christ makes

128

Himself known today through His Spirit, the sin is appropriately titled "Blasphemy of the Holy Spirit." It is understandable that one will have honest historical doubts about the person of Jesus, but ignoring the experience of God's drawing Spirit is quite another matter.

When Christ, by the Spirit's power, performed a miracle in front of certain Pharisees, they were left without an excuse to admit his true identity. Christ's credibility had been clearly established. Not wanting to "knuckle under," the Pharisees quickly attributed the Holy Spirit's work to the power of Satan. This lie is the *blasphemy*. A more modern person might try to write the Spirit's influence off as some kind of weird repressive thought, etc.

It is easy to see why a sinful man does not wish to repent, but is it conceivable that a baby who has not even obtained a sense of right and wrong could possibly commit this sin? Of course not.

...your children who do not yet know good from bad. – *Deuteronomy 1:39*

"But aren't babies inheritors of Adam's sin?"

Yes, in the sense that they are born separated from God and with a nature that will be prone to sin as it grows. The mark of original sin is covered on the cross. The only sin left, "Blasphemy of the Holy Spirit" cannot be committed by a small child.

"At what age can one commit this sin?"

There is no definite answer to that question, for people grow at different paces. Certainly children learn right from wrong early in life, but at what point would God hold them accountable? In my opinion, God waits until a child reaches adulthood. Of course adulthood was at a younger age in the Biblical culture, so by our reckoning it may be somewhere in the teens. They are now starting to try teens as adults when they commit heinous crimes, so our country is admitting that a person is not excused simply for being a minor. But again, since people grow and mature differently, we cannot dogmatically name a cutoff age. For this same reason, I believe God also extends a certain flexibility to those who are mentally handicapped.

CONCLUSION

The purpose of this chapter was to show that people everywhere have a degree of God's light. Because we each have a responsibility to respond to this light, God is completely just in holding people accountable worldwide. Since all have sinned, there is no such thing as the "innocent person who knew nothing of God" (at least, not amongst normal adults). But some are honestly ignorant of the Gospel. I believe God will take that into consideration by judging people according to what they would have done if they *had* heard. God will undoubtedly verify His conclusion by highlighting the manner in which men or women interacted with their own consciences.

---

1 *Impressions of Gandhi* C.F. Andrews, from *The Gandhi Reader*, p. 390. Some may wonder why an awareness of sin did not lead Gandhi to Jesus. One barrier seems to be found in the many Christian hypocrites he encountered. Gandhi was also disappointed when well-meaning Christian friends could not answer even his most basic questions about Christianity. (See *Early Glimpses and Religious Ferment,* both articles by Gandhi, reprinted from Gandhi's autobiography, 1948, Washington Public Affairs Press) Still, Gandhi ultimately rejected the exclusiveness of Hinduism as well, embracing instead a more universal view of religion (*Hinduism* by Gandhi, Oct. 6, 1921 published in *Young Indian*). Whether or not the poor Christian witness around him, contrasted to Gandhi's apparent search for the true God and desire for a cleansed soul qualifies Gandhi on judgment day as "a sincere seeker, ignorant of the Gospel" remains to be seen.

2 Alonzo Bunker, *SooThah, A Tale of the Karens,* (Fleming H. Revell Co. New York, 1902).

3 See Mrs. Macleod Wylie, *The Gospel in Burma,* (W.H Dalton, London, 1859) p. 6.

4 An English diplomat, the first on record to discover the Karen, reported his encounter with the Karen to his superior, Lieutenant Colonel Michael Symes, who mentioned the incident in a writing called *An Account of an Embassy to the Kingdom of Ava in the Year 1795.* See Don Richardson, *Eternity in Their Hearts,* (Regal Books. Ventura California, 1981) p. 73-5.

5 *Ibid.* pp. 73-102.

6 *Ibid.* p. 86 as reported by Alexander MacLeish, Christian Progress in Burma (World Dominion Press, London, 1929) p. 51.

Chapter 8

WHY DID GOD COMMAND THE ISRAELITES TO WIPE OUT OTHER NATIONS?

"Why did God command the Israelites to completely conquer and destroy the other nations who inhabited the land of Canaan, stealing their land and murdering even women and children to the point of mass genocide? How can we serve a God like that or call Him loving?"

Of all the moral challenges to the Bible, this is certainly the hardest to answer, or more correctly put, the hardest to make people understand.

The first part of the question is easier, the question of a God who would command war. God states some pretty good reasons for this in the Scriptures and it is possible for people to track with them. The second part, on a first glance, seems impossible to explain and outrageous in its scope. The very idea of a God who would tell anyone to exterminate an entire race including women and little babies reminds us of the kinds of things Nazis did.

A FAIR BEGINNING

The easier part of the question is the natural place to begin. It is true that after delivering the Hebrews from Egyptian bondage and bringing them to a new home across the desert, God did command the Israelites to wage war against the nations that inhabited the land of Canaan (to which Moses and later Joshua led them to).

However, in the cities of the nations the Lord your God is giving you as an inheritance do not leave alive anything that breathes. Completely destroy them—the Hittites, Amorites, Canaanites, Perizzites, Hivites and Jebusites— as the LORD your God has commanded you. Otherwise they will teach you to follow all the detestable things they do in worshipping their gods, and you will sin against the LORD your God. – Deuteronomy 20:16-18

The reason is stated quite clearly, *"lest they teach you to make any such abominable offerings as they make to their gods and you thus sin against the Lord your God" (v. 18).*

It was common in those days to worship gods by placing babies on the altar, killing them and burning them as an offering. Ironically, the very wars cited by people to accuse the biblical God of a disregard for life were waged against the evil religions and their abominable human destructions that concerned the true, loving God. We see this same problem stated in Leviticus where God commands His people to have nothing to do with evil worship.

Do not give any of your children to be sacrificed to Molech, for you must not profane the name of your God. I am the LORD. – Leviticus 18:21

The LORD said to Moses, "Say to the Israelites: 'Any Israelite or any alien living in Israel who gives any of his children to Molech must be put to death. The people of the community are to stone Him. I will set my face against that man and I will cut him off from his people; for by giving his children to Molech, he has defiled my sanctuary and profaned my holy name. If the people of the community close their eyes when that man gives one of his children to Molech and they fail to put him to death, I will set my face against that man and his family and will cut off from their people both him and all who follow him in prostituting themselves to Molech." – Leviticus 20:1-5

"But didn't the LORD make similar demands? What about Abraham sacrificing Isaac at God's command?"

Abraham was prepared to carry out that order for again, that was a common method of worshipping many gods. However, the lesson of this story is that God was simply testing Abraham's obedience. We must remember how God stopped Him and said: *"Do not lay a hand on the boy."* (Genesis 22:12)

132

"What about the sacrifice of Jephthah's daughter?" (Judges 11)

God never commanded Jephthah to make this sacrifice. It was his own idea, and there is no evidence that God had anything to do with it. Jephthah was typical of people who frequently assume the worst about God and obey commands He didn't even issue. Likewise, in the early years of Christianity, many monks lived on grass and slept fully dressed with belts or chords out of a belief that they were pleasing God by denying themselves pleasure.[1] Although noble in their motives, they were not actually obeying any command of the New Testament, and they may have pleased God just as well by having a fine meal and a good night's sleep.

Returning now to the subject at hand, we have established God's reason for conquering the nations of Canaan; *a concern for human rights*. As the author of life and the supreme judge of the earth, God has every right to deal with evil wherever He sees it. Sending the Israelites to Canaan served a dual purpose, the execution of God's justice and a new home for Israel.

"But if only God has a right to take a life, why would He use people as collaborators?"

God sends forth His wrath in many different ways. Sometimes He does it Himself, as in the destruction of Pharaoh's armies (Exodus 14:23-31). Sometimes He uses angels, as in the destruction of Sodom and Gomorrah (Genesis 18). Sometimes He uses people. The interpretation would have been the same in those days. Any such mode would have been viewed as coming from God. It was believed that each nation had its own deities and that when nations went to war, the gods were in fact fighting behind the scenes. Wars of this sort are shocking to our twentieth century sensibilities, but back then nobody said, "See, those horrible Israelites conquering the land." Instead they said, "Evidently the God of the Israelites is stronger than the gods of the Canaanites. Therefore, the land is theirs." This is a major difference of interpretation.

Let me now share an extremely important observation: It does not make sense that this same God who wants to deliver the babies would then turn around and say to the Israelites (instruments of His justice), "To rescue these babies I want you to kill the entire populace, including all women and children, thus annihilating even more babies." Probably that is not what happened. In all likelihood, there is something we are not catching here—something which does not immediately meet the eye.

"But many Christians say exactly that. They talk about children suffering for the sins of their parents. They justify God's destruction of children by saying that in those days the only way to punish a person was to punish his entire family as well."

It is true that the ancient Middle Eastern cultures held children responsible for the sins of their parents. But this was a belief radically challenged by the Holy Scriptures.

Fathers shall not be put to death for their children, nor children for their fathers. Only for his own guilt shall a man be put to death. – Deuteronomy 24:16

At the time of the kings, Amaziah obeyed this law. He put to death men who killed his father but spared their sons (2 Kings 14:6).

In Ezekiel's day this remained a familiar teaching:

"Yet you ask, 'Why does the son not share the guilt of his father?' Since the son has done what is just and right and has been careful to keep my decrees, he will surely live. The soul who sins is the one who will die. The son will not share the guilt of the father, nor will the father share the guilt of the son. The righteousness of the righteous man will be credited to him and the wickedness of the wicked will be charged against them." – Ezekiel 18:19-20

"But don't we read in the second of the Ten Commandments that sins are passed on to the third and fourth generation?"

Here is the passage:

...for I the Lord your God am a jealous God, punishing the children for the sin of the fathers to the third and fourth generation of those who hate me, but showing love to a thousand generations of those who love me and keep my commandments. – Exodus 20:5-6

"To the third and fourth generation," was a typical Semitic phrase, which addressed at its heart, continuity. This was not to be interpreted as a mathematical equation. It was instead describing the probability that children will follow in the footsteps of their parents.[2]

"Then why was Achan's entire family put to death for his sin of stealing?" (Joshua 7)

In all probability, they participated in the crime. Remember, the ages of his children are not given and his children could have been grown adults still living with their parents, a very common living arrangement in those days.

MOVING ON TO THE HARDER PART

Now that we have established some background, let us return to the second part of the original question: Why did God command the Israelites to completely wipe out the nations of Canaan in mass genocide?

In a nutshell, He didn't. Or at least, a very good case can be made that He didn't. When God commanded the destruction of certain nations, He seems to have meant "displace them as a people" as opposed to "completely exterminate." For one thing, these people all continued to exist hundreds of years later at the time of Solomon:

All the people left from the Hitties, Amorites, Perizzites, Hivites and Jebusites (these people were not Israelites) that is, their descendants remaining in the land, whom the Israelites had not destroyed–these Solomon conscripted for his slave labor force as it is to this day. – 2 Chronicles 8:7-8

135

Notice that every nation listed in Deuteronomy 20 as targets for destruction is listed here with the exception of the Canaanites. Since *Canaan* was a double term referring both to the entire land of Canaan as well as an individual nation within the land, the author of 2 Chronicles may have felt it unnecessary to repeat the term. In any event we know that people of Canaanite nationality survived as well (Matthew 15:22). From this provocative passage in Chronicles we can reach two very safe conclusions:

1) The Israelites obviously did not exterminate these people, for if they had, there would have been few, if any, survivors. Obviously, this is a description meaning more than a handful of fleeing refugees as these are people settled in the land, entrenched enough to retain some of their national identity all the way up through Solomon's time several hundred years later.

2) Solomon himself did not feel he had to exterminate them to "finish the job."

We conclude that conquering the land and enforcing the servitude of the people is all that the Israelites did and all that they understood God commanding them to do.

"Then how do we explain extreme words like 'completely destroy?' "

The Hebrew word *destroy* is charam and means "the irrevocable giving over to God." That can include destruction but it does not necessarily mean *destroy* in the sense we know the word.

There is also an explanation in the way ancient Hebrews and others talked back in those days. They used extreme exaggerated phrases and spoke somewhat poetically a great deal of the time.

The following quote is from Dr. Samuel Davidson, a scholar familiar with the ways of the ancient near east.

"He who does not remember the wide difference between the

Oriental and Occidental mind must necessarily fall into error. The luxuriant imagination and the glowing ardor of the former express themselves in the hyperbolically and extravagant diction, whereas the subdued character and coolness of the latter are averse to sensuous luxuriance."[3]

So at times the commands of God (as regards war) were written in a style that the Hebrews themselves would have taken as exaggerated and poetic. But at other times, the details of the war (sparing women and children) were spelled out. In Deuteronomy 20 we seem to see both used together.

> *When you march up to attack a city, make its people an offer of peace. If they accept and open their gates, all the people in it shall be subject to forced labor and shall now work for you. If they refuse to make peace and they engage you in battle, lay siege to that city. When the Lord your God delivers it into your hand, put to the sword all the men in it. As for the women, the children, the livestock and everything else in the city, you may take these as plunder for yourselves. – Deuteronomy 20:10-14*

Again, God's precautions to avoid innocent casualties of war are noteworthy. Unfortunately, the passage is harder when we read on:

> *However, in the cities of the nations the Lord your God is giving you as an inheritance, do not leave alive anything that breathes. Completely destroy them—the Hittites, Amorites, Canaanites, Perizzites, Hivites and Jebusites as the LORD your God has commanded you. Otherwise they will teach you to follow all the detestable things they do in worshipping their gods, and you will sin against the LORD your God." – Deuteronomy 20:16-18*

We must read this passage in the light of all that we have learned:

1. The Israelites did not in fact completely destroy those nations, but instead displaced them as a people.
2. God does not punish children for the sins of their parents. Indeed, it is out of a concern for children that He was using the

137

Hebrews to conquer those people anyway.

3. The sparing of women and children seems a standard practice issued by God.
4. The word for *destroy* could be interpreted as "completely give over to God," a phrase compatible with the notion of conquering.
5. The Hebrews often spoke in exaggerated phrases.

For all these reasons, I have come to the conclusion that the sparing of women and children discussed in the first part of this passage is *assumed* in the second part. The contrast between the two commands is in the fact that with some cities peace will be offered and men accepting the offer can be spared, but in those cities inhabiting the land of Canaan, peace will not be offered. The adult males of those cities are to be executed, for from them the practice of other religious worship would spread, whereas with women and children, the bondage and servitude would be more readily accepted. The phrase "put to death everything that breathes," extreme and poetic in its rhythm, would be a way of saying, "Put to death the males, the authorities, and in so doing you are destroying the nation for all intents and purposes."[4]

Many dedicated Christians will disagree with my conclusion. Although the idea of exaggerated Hebrew speech is a fact of history, it is not always clear when these exaggerations are taking place, and I therefore completely respect those who read this passage differently. It is also pointed out by many that if God wants to completely destroy a nation, He is at liberty to do so. After all, He is a just God whose decisions need to be trusted rather than criticized, and we with our sinful natures may simply have a hard time seeing how a holy God chooses to do things. This is an idea I can accept. My point above is that we don't necessarily have to read some of those passages as we may have previously thought.

"But however we read the passages, even if we take the view that God wanted the children spared, isn't it true that in any war, children are likely to die, even by accident? So by commanding these wars God knew that at least some children would die."

138

This very understandable question was expressed to me publicly during an open forum at Oregon State University. I knew that the student would initially reject my answer, but I threw it out anyway. "According to the New Testament (Matthew 12), all children who die at an early age go to Heaven and in Heaven they will continue to live with God. In fact, they will be much better off than they were on earth living with evil parents who sacrificed babies on the altar."

"Oh sure, that old cop-out answer," the student complained. "Talking about Heaven is a very convenient thing to say."

"When discussing Heaven," I replied, "you must ask yourself what you truly believe. If you don't accept the Bible as being factual when it discusses Heaven, why accept the Bible as factual when it discusses war?"

Once again, we return to our original premise, a moral question about the Bible. These questions only remain fair within the boundaries of their assumptions:

Question: Assuming that the Bible is the Word of God, isn't it unfair that God commanded wars in which children died?

Answer: Assuming that the Bible is the Word of God, those children are in Heaven and they are very happy. They are not screaming at God for bringing them there.

MODERN DAY APPLICATIONS

"Couldn't the belief in Old Testament Holy Wars inspire Christians to do violence in the name of God?"

Christians are commanded to live by the New Testament, not the Old Testament. Jesus made it clear that under this New Covenant, couriers of the Gospel would be instruments of God's mercy, rather than God's wrath. He discouraged any kind of violent overthrow of the Roman empire (Matthew 22:21) and said, "...all who draw the sword will die by the sword" (Matthew 26:52). God has always been a God of both mercy and wrath. What has changed under the New Covenant is our rapport with God. Previously God used His people as instruments of His judgment, but today, we reflect the attribute of mercy as God saves His wrath for judgment day. Jesus warned against merging the Old and New Covenant together, comparing it to the mixture of new wine with old wineskins (Luke 5:37-38).

Many disturbing events of Church history, such as the Crusades and the Inquisition, show the fallacy and horror of attempts to spread the New Testament Gospel through Old Testament methods. However, as mentioned in our discussion of hypocrisy in Chapter 1, such deeds were done in disobedience to the teachings of Jesus.

CONCLUSION

Although God did command the Israelites to make war upon the nations living in Canaan, He did this to judge the evil in those nations. It is unlikely that God commanded the entire genocide of the nations and on the bottom line there was no such genocide because the nations continued to exist. Still, there would have been some innocent casualties of war, and when we see such things we are grateful for the hope of the resurrection.

---

1 See Kenneth Scott Latourette, *A History of Christianity Volume I* (Harper and Row, New York, Hagerstown, San Francisco, London, 1975) p. 228, and *Rules of St. Benedict* as reprinted in Henry Bettenson, *Documents of the Christian Church* (Oxford University Press, London, Oxford, New York, 1978) p. 118.

2 Alan Cole, a professor at Macquaire University Australia, discusses this in detail in his book, *Exodus.*

3 Dr. Samuel Davidson, *Introduction to the Old Testament,* p. 409.

4 I believe this argument is made even more conclusive when we remember that Joshua, after conquering the land of Canaan, was said to have obeyed everything the Lord commanded him to do.

Joshua 11:15—As the Lord commanded his servant Moses, so Moses commanded Joshua, and Joshua did it; he left nothing undone of all that the Lord commanded Moses.

Chapter 9

IS THE BIBLE A CHAUVINISTIC BOOK?

"Isn't the Bible kind of backwards and behind the times where the roles of men and women are concerned? How can I take seriously any document that teaches a wife to obey her husband like some kind of slave? How can I respect commands which insist that women refrain from leadership in the church?"

You have certainly expressed a common and serious concern. But have you considered the possibility that this may not be an authentic problem with the Bible, but rather with the way many Christians are interpreting the Bible? Sincere and well-meaning people often read passages out of context.[1]

APPRAISING THE COMMON CHRISTIAN VIEW

It was a Christian advertisement for a Christian bookstore being broadcast over (you guessed it) a Christian radio station. According to the friendly commercial, *Grace Reading* was no ordinary run – of-the-mill bookstore. They had more than just books. They had items that would be of interest to women also.

"For you men, commentaries, concordances, Greek Lexicons. For you women, perfume, jewelry, and praise tapes."

True story; extreme example. Still, it tells us something about how today's market views women. Unfortunately, it also helps explain our culture's current viewpoint of Christianity, namely that Christianity is several light-years behind the times.

When conducting evangelistic dialogues on college campuses, I am inevitably faced with the question: "Is the Bible a chauvinistic book?"

While attempting to answer, "No, actually Jesus and the apostles were very liberating," I am frequently interrupted and "assisted" by some helpful Christian in the audience who explains that although God will of course love men and women equally, women must be under the spiritual covering of a man. Spiritual Covering is an interesting expression. Interesting because I'm convinced that nobody really knows what this overused buzz phrase means.

"It's so frustrating," I've heard many women say, "that my husband doesn't assert himself as the leader of our household. Indeed, I am more interested in spiritual things than he is and I know that isn't right."

Hmm. That is a problem for sure. The very audacity of a woman being more interested in spiritual things than a man. Why did she grow so fast? However did she get ahead of her husband? Who dared to disciple her so well? What an assault on the cosmic order!

Is it possible that these mandates of male leadership are putting undue pressure on both men and women? People usually do feel pressure when they submit to principles that don't make any sense. Just imagine. Some poor man just gave his life to Jesus. All of a sudden he's supposed to be his wife's spiritual leader.

"Can somebody explain this?" I like to ask, "Are men closer to God than women? Do men have more of the Holy Spirit than women?"

"No," is the typical conservative answer.

"Well, are men more intelligent than women?" "No."

"Then why must women be in submission to men?"

"Because the Bible says so."

The Bible. O.K., at least there is some hope for objective discussion. The Bible is a common ground for settling differences of opinion between Evangelical Christians. Some movements in Christianity (such as the liberal movement) deal with hot topics by assuming that the Bible is not completely the word of God. They believe the apostles may be mistaken in many of their teachings, including their teaching on marriage. *This is not an option for me.* Instead, I acknowledge that two people believing in the authority of Scripture can come away with different conclusions. I do not see this as a problem with the way the Bible was written, but rather as a human problem since our biases sometimes keep us from viewing the Scripture in its proper context.

SOME CONTROVERSIAL PASSAGES

Now it's true that the Bible contains some very crisp imperatives about the submission of women. Wives are commanded to obey their husbands and women are forbidden to teach in the Church.

> *Wives, submit to your husbands as to the Lord. For the husband is the head of the wife as Christ is the head of the church, his body, of which He is the Savior. – Ephesians 5:22-23*

> *I do not permit a woman to teach or to have authority over a man. She must remain silent. – 1 Timothy 2:12*

Many who do not like these verses try to imagine that Paul and the others didn't quite say what they seemed to say: "Maybe being a leader means being a servant." "Maybe Paul is just talking about an attitude." Those holding the patriarchal view find it difficult to respect this kind of cut and snip job on scripture. In their minds, it verifies what they suspected all along, Egalitarians are not being honest with the Bible.

Personally, I consider it a waste of time to argue about whether these troublesome commands say what they mean and mean what they say. Obviously they do. Even a third grader could tell us that words are clear. Instead, we should ask ourselves *why* the Bible issues such commands.

I find it quite interesting that the passages commanding wives to obey their husbands are found right next to passages about slaves obeying their masters. If we keep reading in Ephesians it says;

> *Slaves, obey your earthly masters with respect and fear and with sincerity of heart just as you would obey Christ. – Ephesians 6:5*

143

Not only is this found shortly after the husband/wife passage but it uses a similar analogy with our relationship to Christ.

In Colossians and 1 Peter, the commands are also found together. This doesn't surprise me, for in the ancient world, women were generally viewed as the property of men. One could purchase a wife very much the way he purchased a slave. Marriage was essentially a form of slavery.[2]

Could we justify slavery today? When we read passages such as "Slaves obey your masters" do we not assume that Paul had some unique reason for his unusual request? If we were to take those passages at face value, out of context, we might conclude that God condones the idea of owning another human being. But this would be a false conclusion. After all, Paul made it clear that slave trading was an evil practice (I Timothy 1:10).

How then, do we handle this apparent contradiction? We may actually find a clue by first observing a different apostle. In 1 Peter 2-3, Peter explained that as far as God is concerned, Christians have been liberated from all earthly institutions, including the institution of slavery. However, for the sake of testimony, Peter still insisted that submission to these institutions continue. Evidently he did not want the peaceful revolution of Christ to be spoiled by a violent revolution. At the time of his writing, Rome had more slaves than citizens. Declaring the slaves free would have been no less than declaring war on Rome, something Jesus, his Lord and Savior, refused to do (Matthew 22:15-22).

If this was Peter's approach, it makes sense that Paul would have a similar strategy. After all, this is the same Paul who bridged the gap between Jew and Gentile (Acts 15), who instructed Christians to respect each other's differences of opinion (Romans 14), and who took a vow he considered unnecessary just to preserve the peace with fellow Jewish Christians (Acts 21:20-26). Finally, it is the best explanation for his opposite statements about slavery;

Were you a slave when you were called? Don't let it trouble you, although if you can gain your freedom, do so. – 1 Corinthians 7:21

But perhaps Paul's most liberating text is found in Galatians 3:28: *There is neither Jew nor Greek, slave nor free, male nor female, for you are all one in Christ Jesus.*

Paul is describing three strong social distinctions of his day. *What's interesting to me is that Christians seem to understand the elimination of the first two classes as they hold on to the third.* Imagine someone coming into the church and listening to an orientation that says, "In our church there is no racial division. Israel may have been a chosen nation by God but Gentiles are now a part of this Israel spiritually and in our church we recognize no difference between Jews and Gentiles; however, only Jews can be in positions of leadership. Got that? We are all equal before God, but only Jews can preach."

Does that sound ridiculous? How about this? A church introduction in ancient Rome: "When you enter these walls you leave the world behind. Out in the world, slaves and masters exist. In here, there is no such order. We have neither slave nor free for we are one in Christ; however, I'm sure you can understand, slaves do not teach in our church."

Sound crazy? Of course, because our present day American culture has long since abolished the institution of slavery and our hindsight shows us how horrible it was. We recognize these Bible commands about slaves obeying their masters as temporary limited injunctions due to the special situation of Ancient Rome. For Paul's clear theology of slavery we turn to his liberating teaching in Galatians (as seen above).

Of course, only a little over a hundred years ago right here in this very same America, the Pre-Civil war south would have still been wrestling with slavery. My point is this: Much as we'd like to think that one can open the Bible and simply read it, we are all influenced by our cultures and today's Christian sub-culture has not yet settled the gender issue. Certainly one can read the Bible without the interpretation of a pastor or teacher, but all too often that is not what happens. Christians are not used to cold readings of certain passages. Instead, they are used to expositions of these passages, and most verses about the submission of women have not been approached in the same manner as the

145

slavery issue, although, as demonstrated above, this would be a more consistent method of interpretation.

"But I have heard many Christians describe a difference between gender-based submission and slavery? 'After all,' they say, 'God created men and women differently.' "

There are differences, but nobody knows for sure what these differences are (aside from the obvious physical and biological differences).

I can discuss politics with a woman, and she may make all the same points that a man would make. Still, the conversation has a different feel because I am talking to a woman. This intuition can be accepted without the temptation to analyze and figure out what the differences are. We walk off a cliff when we try to define the differences. For example, many will say that women *feel* more than men and men *think* more than women. The Margaret Thatchers and Amelia Earharts of the world seem to dispel this notion. So do the "feeling-oriented" men in the Bible like David, Jeremiah, and even Jesus, men who were not shy about showing their tears and other strong emotions (Psalm 6:7-8; Jeremiah 13:17; John 11:35).

But again, without the analysis, we still conclude some undefined differences between men and women. The question remains: Does a difference forbid leadership? After all, we have different leadership gifts in the Church (prophet, teacher, apostle, pastor), and children need both a father and mother. Indeed, Deborah the prophet was called the mother of Israel (Judges 5:7) because she ruled her people for some 40 years. The frequent rebuttal says she did this only because no man would take the job. This is an argument based upon silence, for the Bible does not say anything of the kind.

Going back to Creation, the only description of submission comes after the fall when men and women were cursed separately. Adam's curse was that work would lose its fulfillment and be filled with drudgery. As for Eve's curse,

"I will greatly increase your pains in childbearing: with pain you will give birth to children. Your desire will be for your husband, and he will rule over you." – Genesis 3:16

I have to assume that if obedience to her husband was some kind of new curse, then obviously back in the garden prior to the curse, Eve was not living under a mandate to obey Adam.

"But according to your Bible, we still live under the curse, so shouldn't women still obey their husbands?"

Christ's death and resurrection started a process which will eventually do away with the effects of the curse (Galatians 3:13-14). In Heaven, women and men will be joint heirs, kings and priests (Galatians 3:29; 1 Peter 2:9). We conclude that women were co-rulers with men before the curse and that women will continue to be co-rulers after the Second Coming of Christ when the curse is completely abolished. It is the present in-between time that raises questions.

"O.K. Well then let's concentrate on the present in-between time. Work is still difficult and women certainly experience pain in child-bearing, so the curse is still in operation. Therefore, if Christians want to take the Bible seriously, women should still obey men."

Yes, the curse is still here because Christ's Kingdom has only begun to enter the world and will not reach fruition until the Second Coming. But the church still represents the Kingdom of God here on earth. In other words, we model the ideal, not the curse. When men receive spiritual gifts and do works of ministry, are they not fulfilled with a sense of the enjoyable and important? The very word for gift (charisma) comes from the Greek word *char* which means *joy*. Therefore, the curse of unhappy work for men has been at least partly eradicated. What right do we have to say that the church will try to free men from their curse but leave women to remain under theirs?

"Then why does Paul forbid women to even speak in church?"

As in all the congregations of the saints, women should remain silent in the churches. They are not allowed to speak, but must be in submission as the Law says. If they want to inquire about something, they should ask their own husbands at home, for it is disgraceful for a woman to speak in the church. – 1 Corinthians 14:34-35

We know Paul *did not* forbid women to speak because he already told us in this very same letter that women could pray and prophesy in church (1 Corinthians 11). Remember, a prophet was one of the five authoritative offices listed in Ephesians 4. Paul's topic here in 1 Corinthians 14 is order in the worship service. He had already expressed concern about tongues without an interpretation and prophets who interrupted each other. Now he asks women to save their questions instead of speaking out of turn. The early church modeled their services after the Jewish synagogue, where men and women sat on separate sides.3 For women to ask their husbands questions, they would actually have to shout across the room. It is easy to understand how disruptive that could be. Therefore, Paul isn't objecting to the education of women. He is instead asking them to wait for the appropriate time.

"But there is another passage where Paul forbids women to teach. How is this one explained?"

A woman should learn in quietness and full submission. I do not permit a woman to teach or to have authority over a man; she must be silent. For Adam was formed first, then Eve. And Adam was not the one deceived; it was the woman who was deceived and became a sinner. But women will be kept safe through childbirth, if they continue in faith, love and holiness with propriety. – 1 Timothy 2:11-15

Some might argue from this passage that Paul's illustration of Adam and Eve takes us as far out of the Grecian-Roman world as we can get, and therefore, we must view this not as a temporary injunction, but rather as a universal command for all time. Although I sympathize with such an observation, a lot can be said in response.

Keep in mind that 1 Timothy is actually a letter. When we read it, we are reading somebody else's mail. Even though it is a part of the Bible and the inspired Word of God, *we are not reading Paul's teaching on the role of women*. We are instead reading *some reminders of things he had already taught Timothy in person*. We also seem to be reading answers to some specific questions Timothy raised in an earlier letter and this letter, unfortunately, has been lost.

Here's another matter for consideration: We cannot hear Paul's tones as we read his words. We don't know where he would be accentuating his expression. The absence of such accents can sometimes cause us to read a passage in a manner unintended by the author.

As an example, let's look at the illustration of the optimist and the pessimist. The pessimist sees the glass of water as half empty while the optimist sees it as half full. When Paul says the women should learn in silence and submission, people immediately latch onto the *silence and submission part*, forgetting that Paul is still encouraging the education of women, something virtually unheard of in those days. For the church to be educating women was as radical and egalitarian as an institution could get. Timothy had undoubtedly raised some questions about the practice of instructing females in spiritual matters. Evidently, the women were getting impatient and not showing respect to the men who were discipling them. This may have intimidated the men, causing them to re-evaluate this new universal freedom in Christ.

Timothy evidently asked Paul to clarify his previous instructions. "Did you really want us to teach women? It sure is causing a problem." Paul responds by saying, "The women *should* learn." Notice how the thrust of the word *should* changes with an accent as indicated in the italics. Again, we don't know Paul's tone, but we must admit that it is possible to read this passage much differently than the conventional way. Women were being educated according to their new freedom in Christ, but the fact is, they had been kept in the dark for so many years that presently they were uneducated and, as a result, not yet qualified to teach.

As we continue to examine Paul's words, several pertinent questions will surface.

1. Is Paul really teaching that women are more easily deceived then men? If so, why does he encourage women to teach other women (Titus 2:4)? If it's dangerous for a man to be taught by a woman, why isn't it dangerous for a woman to be taught by a woman?

2. What does childbirth have to do with a discussion of submission? They seem like two completely different subjects.

It is interesting that Paul should throw in this all new discussion out of the blue. Not only does it seem to come from nowhere, but it doesn't make any sense. Do we really believe women are saved by having children? Isn't the very notion rather ludicrous and inconsistent with the New Testament's plain teaching about salvation? To answer these questions, we must try to find another place in Scripture where the subjects of submission and childbirth were lumped together. Actually, there is one other place, and interestingly enough, it too involves Adam and Eve.

I will greatly increase your pains in childbearing: with pain you will give birth to children. Your desire will be for your husband, and he will rule over you. – Genesis 3:16

We have established that part of Eve's curse was a submission to her husband that she did not experience back in the Garden and that she will no longer experience in the restored Kingdom of Christ. In my opinion, the only reason Paul could possibly have for discussing childbirth at this juncture, is to remind his readers that the submissive state of women is a cursed state, a state of which she is being saved from.

But women will be kept safe through childbirth, if they continue in faith, love and holiness with propriety (1 Timothy 3:14).

150

The word *through* (dia) is the same word used in 1 Corinthians 3: 15: He himself will be saved but only as *through* flames i.e., you are being saved out of a fiery process. Likewise, Paul could be talking about a delivery from the curse of which pain in childbirth is one aspect and submission to men is another.

> **"O.K. This explains part of Paul's usage of Adam and Eve but not all of it. How come Paul says that women can't teach because Adam was formed first?"**

If order of Creation were that important to God, then all of us should be in submission to animals for they were created before people. A very common method of interpreting Scripture in Paul's day was the allegorical method used by the Jewish Midrash.4 Paul, having been a Rabbi himself, was familiar with this practice. Sometimes Old Testament stories were used to draw analogous points.
We have biblical precedent for this in Galatians 4:21-31 where Paul compares Sarah and Hagar to heavenly Jerusalem and earthly Jerusalem. Likewise, he may be using a Midrash idea here, as if to say, "As Adam was formed first, then Eve, so men were educated first, but be of good cheer, women are being educated now."

It seems that Paul is simply reminding the men and women to be patient. Women are being delivered from the effects of the curse, including the submissive effect. They are being educated. But in the process of education, men, like Adam were formed first, so the women must be patient.

Can I prove this interpretation of the passage? No. Is it possible and plausible according to principles of sound hermeneutics? Yes. How, then, do we make our final decision? Ultimately, by asking ourselves which interpretation fits the context of other Scripture. A Patriarchal view of 1 Timothy 2 directly contradicts Paul's plain teaching on the equality of men and women. If we have a plausible interpretation which fits the flow of other scripture, this becomes the suitable interpretation.

"If this really is a valid way to interpret Scripture, why are there so few egalitarian Christians?"

Obviously I can't speak for everybody. I do know that many people are hesitant to embrace the egalitarian viewpoint out of a fear that it supports the current feminist movement with its anti-male agenda. Such concern is understandable but unnecessary. We need to be careful not to assume guilt by association. Certainly some feminists may appreciate my approach to Scripture. But this does not mean that I embrace everything about the feminist movement. Any teaching which sows discord among the sexes would certainly be incompatible with Christianity. When the feminist movement began, it was simply about equality. For some feminist leaders it has become more than that, and unfortunately a lot of male bashing has taken place. I can only wonder what may have happened if the church had been the forerunner of a balanced and loving feminist revolution; one which sought equality of the sexes without the antagonism.

SUMMARY

Contrary to being a chauvinistic book, the Bible in many places speaks of the liberation of women. Still, because the Bible comes out of a chauvinistic culture, this may be the reason why the education of women was a slow process the men in the church needed to get used to. Although the Bible gives some clear commands to women in the area of submission, it is very difficult not to at least consider the possibility that these gender commands were temporary, limited statements due to the existing situation of the ancient world.

We cannot prove this viewpoint to be the correct interpretation. But neither can one be positive that the commands are for all time, especially when we admit that other commands such as slave submission were not meant for all time.

If we are uncertain, let's give women the benefit of the doubt. Surely God will understand a people who move as far from the curse and as close to the ideal as possible.

1 Some may wonder why I included this chapter, for it deals with an issue of hot disagreement amongst Christians. Sincere Christians have held varying degrees of opinion on this subject for years and certainly my modest little chapter will not settle the debate. But this is an issue of grave concern to many unbelievers. They view the Bible as oppressive and demeaning to women. Since I wrote my book primarily for them, I wanted to remove this barrier by helping people to see an alternative way to interpret certain passages about women, an alternative which may pleasantly surprise them. This does not mean that I have an agenda or that I am insisting people agree with me. And it certainly does not mean that I disrespect those who take more conservative positions on this theology. What then is my point? If the gender issue is the primary setback to investigating Jesus, it may be refreshing to hear of a different approach to the subject. That's all.

Some would say that the differences amongst Christians disprove my earlier point in Chapter Four about the human conscience agreeing with the Bible's commands. Actually they don't. I doubt that anybody (even one with a Patriarchal view) could look into the human conscience and find an impulse which suggests that women should be subservient to men. However, Christians will put the Word of God above their feelings, as well they should. When this chapter explores whether the submission commands were permanent or temporary it is easy to see that this is mostly a matter of theology, not morality. Christians disagree frequently on theology for two reasons: a) On some subjects, the Bible does not give enough information with which to be dogmatic. This is one such subject. b) People too quickly trust the teachings of their pastors without always studying the Bible for themselves. For a fuller treatment about Christians and pastors from this author, see *A Call to Radical Discipleship* (Mission to the Americas, Wheaton, Illinois, 1997) p.79-95.

One final observation relating to Chapter 4: If we really are living under one command (Matthew 7:12), then an even better case is made for the egalitarian position. When one asks about the command for women to submit, I respond by saying, "What command? Christians do not have a series of laws. We are now free from law and we live under Jesus' one Golden Rule through the Holy Spirit."

2 The New Testament comes from a unique time in history when the Jewish, Greek, and Roman cultures converged to a large extent in many places. For this reason, we should study how each of these three cultures treated women.

The Jewish Talmud tells us that money was one of three ways to acquire a woman. Deed and intercourse are the other two ways (*Kiddushin 2a, Babylonian Talmud*). Ancient Rabbis also interpreted Exodus 20:17 as references to property (*Mishna Ketuboth 4:6 and 6:1, Palestinian Talmud*).

In ancient Rome, women were purchased if they came from the lower class. With upper class women, a special dowry arrangement was made when a man took a wife, but the woman still had no choice in the matter. (Will Durant, *Caesar and Christ*, p. 57) The ancient writer Plutarch tells us that husbands had control over the lives and educations of their wives (*Conjugal Precepts, from Essays and Miscellanies* pp. 4, 48, 29, 11, 33, 16) Clough and Goodwin, translators)

The ancient Greek writer Xenophon said that marriage was arranged for women at an early age to men they did not know (*Within the Home*, p. 626, Greek Reader translation).

3 Clement, in his letter to the Corinthians, written early in the second century, tells us that early services were based on the worship of the Jews and modeled after the synagogue. The ancient Jewish commentator Philomentions a structure which separated men and women in the synagogue (*On the Contemplative Life*, vs. 32).

4 The Midrash was influenced evidently by the writings of Philo, who made the allegorical method of interpretation popular. Although Philo's allegories usually ended up turning the Bible into Greek philosophy (ex. *On the Unchangeableness of God*, 131-135), the allegorical method itself left its mark on the Midrash. See Rabbah 1:1 for an example in the Midrash of an allegorical interpretation of Psalm 103:20. "You mighty ones who do his bidding" is said to refer to Jews who obey the Sabbatical year, despite the fact that they still owed a land tax to the Romans.

Conclusion

Our Post-Modern culture has a tendency to talk about truth as though it were a passing fad, emphasizing instead personal or relative truth, but people in fact, live their lives by assuming the existence of objective reality. Regardless of the popular creed or the fashionable lingo, our Freudian slips reveal our honest convictions. Deep in the caverns of their hearts, people *do* accept right and wrong, God and judgment, truth and falsehood.

My purpose was to help the reader apply these convictions to Christianity. This was a difficult task, not because of any genuine problem with the Bible, but because of our tendency as human beings to respond to images and pop descriptions. Today, Christianity has a reputation for being fanciful, dogmatic, prejudiced, and suppressive. I hope this book has gone some distance to show how undeserved that reputation is. Perhaps, at a first glance, Christianity looks far too incredible to swallow. Certainly the notion of Jesus Christ being the only true God or the only way of salvation sounds bizarre, but in the final analysis, we aren't really interested in sounds. We're interested in facts and reasons.

Whether you stumbled upon this book at the beginning or middle of your search, I realize that one volume of literature can only be a small part of your quest. I hope you will continue to study these areas where we only scratched the surface.
More importantly, I hope you will seek God through prayer. But whatever you decide to do from here on out and whatever your final conclusions, I do commend you for the openness it took to consider my case. With sincere wishes, I will pray that you soon discover the limitless treasure which I and others have graciously received.

Appendix: Special Section on Josephus' Testimonium Flavianum

The earliest Greek copy of Antiquities 18 (designated as A) dates around the eleventh century. There is a Latin translation which dates much earlier (sixth century). Since by this time the works of Josephus were in the hands of the Christians, and since these manuscripts are so far removed in time from the originals, it is easy for some to assert that Christians doctored up the passages.

A pertinent question to start off this discussion is this: Why would Christians with such an ambition restrict themselves to one short paragraph and not just forge a whole chapter or book about Jesus allegedly written by Josephus?[1]

I must also point out that scholars do not have much problem with anything else written by Josephus despite the fact that these too are copies and not originals. Most of what we have from the ancient world is copied, and this is not considered cause for alarm amongst scholars, unless the manuscripts seem to verify Christianity. Then whole new standards are usually applied.[2]

But here is what's really interesting: If the passage got doctored up, the alteration would have to have taken place long before our earliest extant manuscripts, and as we are about to see, this would have been difficult. We know that Eusebius (A.D. 260-339) was familiar with the *Testimonium Flavianum* in the same form as copies A and Lat. He is the first author on record to mention it. In two of his writings he quotes the passage word for word (*Ecclesiastical History l:11 and Demonstration. Evan.* Lib iii p 124). In a third, he mentions it with minor variations (*Proof of the Gospel* 3:5). Eusebius is bridging a tremendous gap, and I believe that by briefly comparing the history of his writings with the history of Josephus, we find very little window of opportunity for manuscript tampering.

Considered a traitor by the Jews for surrendering to Vespasian in battle after unsuccessfully leading a Jewish revolt (A.D. 67), Josephus was granted protection from this Roman General who later on became Emperor. Living in Rome under the wing of the Emperor, Josephus became quite popular, so popular that many people began to copy and circulate his books. Christians did this too because Josephus had a good, readable, Greek summary of Jewish history at a time when copies of the Holy Scriptures were not as readily available to the public. It is during this time of Christian circulation that the inserted or tampered *Testimonium Flavianum* would have to have come on the horizon since any theory which places it after Eusebius would not be able to explain why Eusebius quotes from the passage in its present form. Unfortunately for the "tampering theory" there is no mention of this passage by Christian writers prior to Eusebius, so once again we are faced with that famous argument from silence.[3]

This theory is also unlikely given the credentials of Eusebius. A clergyman who attended the historical Council of Nicea and returned home as a member of the orthodox majority, Eusebius was commissioned by Constantine, the first Christian Emperor of Rome to deliver an oration commemorating the Tricennalia, the celebration of Constantine's first thirty years as Emperor (335 – 36). After the death of Constantine, Eusebius worked on his biography and was still writing it when he passed away himself. Apparently Constantine admired Eusebius greatly and confided in him about many things.

Eusebius' *History of the Church* dates about 324-25 A.D., and most of it was written about a decade earlier. Since this work was penned shortly after Christianity was legalized and since Eusebius enjoyed favor from Constantine, he would have had access to the most official (and presumably original) texts of Josephus as they had remained in the hands of the Romans, not the church.

We have now established that Eusebius at least had the opportunity for accuracy. The only question remaining is whether he chose to utilize this opportunity or instead purposely changed the *Testimonium Flavianum* to advance some personal agenda. The latter is most doubtful. We must remember that for him to become a reputed historian of his day, some measure of honesty and integrity must have been awarded him. Keep in mind also that he was writing and quoting Josephus for his contemporaries. Since the works of Josephus were distributed to the populace, it would have been very difficult to simply invent some passage out of thin air when too many were around with Josephus manuscripts to contradict him. For this reason, even many scholars who believe some tampering took place, feel that the *Testimonium Flavianum* represents a changed form of a genuine Josephus writing. Some believe that words like *so called* originally appeared before the word *Christ* or *allegedly* before the claim of resurrection and that these phrases were dropped in the passage of time.[4] There are some quotes of the *Testimonium* from other church officials following Eusebius which do show different renderings with words of that sort. But why would Eusebius remove explanatory words? His reference to the passage as it is suggests that he viewed Josephus as one who implied such amendments anyway (without feeling the need to write them), for he refers to Josephus not as a Christian but as a Jewish source. He seems to see Josephus as a historian who is writing about what people claimed and not numbering himself as a follower.

> However, it may not be amiss if over and above, we make use of Josephus the Jew for a further witness (*Dem. Evan.* Lib. iii p.124, William Whiston translation, *The Complete Works of Josephus*, Kregal Publications, Grand Rapids Michigan, 1981, p. 639).

The "alteration theory" presupposes that Eusebius would have dropped such phrases as *so called* to make Josephus more of a believer. Again, that seems counter-productive to Eusebius' purpose in making the quote. It also fails to explain why Eusebius, if he had such an agenda, would not have also reconstructed the Antiquities 20 passage in which Josephus does say "Jesus, who was *called* Christ."

Still, since after Eusebius, different forms of the passage did pop up, let us look at some of the different wordings over the centuries and see if we can account for the variations.

Jerome (332-420) uses a version in Latin that does come close to the standard text, with the exception of the phrase, "He was believed to be the Messiah" (*Of Illustrious Men 13*, as quoted by Steve Mason,

Josephus and the New Testament, Hendrickson Publishers, Peabody Massachusetts,1992, p.168).

Agapius, a tenth century Christian author, writing a history of the world in Arabic, quotes the passage in the following way:

> At this time there was a wise man who was called Jesus. His conduct was good and (He) was known to be virtuous. And many people from among the Jews and the other nations became his disciples. Pilate condemned Him to be crucified and to die. But those who became his disciples did not abandon his discipleship. They reported that He had appeared to them three days after his crucifixion and that He was alive; accordingly He was perhaps the Messiah concerning whom the prophets have recounted wonders. (Brought to light by Shlomo Pines in his book *An Arabic Version of the Testimonium, Flavianum and its Implications, Jerusalem: Israel Academy of Sciences and Humanities*, 1971, pp. 9-10).

At the end of the twelfth century, Michael, the Patriarch of Antioch also quotes from Josephus saying that Jesus "was thought to be the Messiah. But not according to the principal men of our nation" (Relevant portion of the text given by Pines Arabic Version, p. 26).

I am intrigued that people cite these variations to refute the *Testimonium*, for my observation is that they do quite the opposite. It should be pointed out that the quotes differ even from each other. This does not seem to suggest a reference to an earlier, more accurate text. On the contrary, it implies that Josephus simply called Jesus the Messiah and these men in their paraphrases are telling us what they think Josephus meant when he said it. Notice the variations:

— "was thought to be the Messiah"

— "accordingly, he was perhaps the Messiah"

— "He was believed to be the Messiah"

Of course we are reading quotes and not transcriptions for a new manuscript. People frequently paraphrase when they are simply intending to give a quick quote. The literary observation is that these were alternate elaborations, stemming from an earlier simpler statement. Assuming it was common knowledge that Josephus was not a Christian and assuming that he still referred to Jesus as the Messiah, it makes sense that some paraphrases would try to tell us what Josephus "truly intended to say."

Other church authorities over the years referred to the *Testimonium*, citing Josephus as a Jew and not as Christian. He is mentioned by Ambrose (A.D. 360), Hedsronym (A.D. 400), and Isidorus Pelusiota (A.D. 410). Sozomen, (History Eccles Lob. 1 cap. 1440 A.D.) writes:

> Now he seems to me by this revelation almost to proclaim that Christ is God. However, he appears to have been so affected with the strangeness of the thing as to run as it were in a sort of middle way so as not to put any indignity upon believers in Him, but rather to afford his suffrage to them. (William Whiston translation, Ibid. p. 641).

> *Trithemius* (A.D. 1480 Abbas d Scripture Eccles.) says,

> Josephus the Jew, although he continued to be Jew, did frequently commend the Christians and in the Eighteenth book of his Antiquities wrote down an eminent testimony concerning our Lord Jesus Christ (Whiston translation, Ibid, p. 643).

These commentaries over the ages give no hint whatsoever of a belief in a Christian Josephus. If the church had tried to rewrite the Testimonium for that reason, there is absolutely no evidence to support it. On the bottom line, even if it is someday proven that the original Josephus text included words like *was thought* or *perhaps*, we have lost nothing in our argument for it would still show that the resurrection claim was an event monumental enough for a historian to take note of it, trying as hard as he could to refrain from personal bias.

---

1 An Old Russian version of a different book of Josephus, *History of the Jewish War,* contains

a longer passage about Jesus which some believe to be an expanded version of the *Antiquities* passage, proving a Christian interpolation. Interpolations did sometimes happen. They are evident in different versions of the New Testament. In such cases there were a variety of reasons, generally relating to well-meaning scribes who were attempting to explain some unusual word or inconsistency. Sometimes comments that were originally intended as footnotes got into the actual text by mistake. Other times, a scribe truly thought he was correcting an error (since the manuscript he was copying from was also a copy and not the original). But the careful and intellectually faithful scribes far outweighed the presumptuous ones, and the multiple copies of manuscripts can usually show when copyist changes (deliberate or intentional) were made, helping us to reconstruct, with considerable accuracy, what the original manuscript said. This discipline, known as Textual Criticism is explained with great detail by Princeton Professor, Bruce Metzger in *The Text of the New Testament, Its Transmission, Corruption, and Restoration* (Oxford University Press, New York, 1992).

With this in mind, let me make a few observations about the Slavonic Josephus passage. First of all, it does not have the manuscript verification of the *Testimonium* for it comes up in only one manuscript (dated eleventh or twelfth century) and is not found in any Greek editions of *History of the Jewish War*. Therefore, this time we have good objective evidence that something was added. No such case can be made for the *Testimonium*.

In any event, this Slavonic version, (however it got there) takes a very neutral position on who Jesus was and instead gives detail about His trial. Such reporting suggests that it may not be an expanded version of the *Testimonium* at all but perhaps another historical tradition about Jesus, (maybe from Josephus, maybe from some anonymous author) that floated around independently for a while and that somebody eventually included into Josephus' writings.

I do not dismiss the fact that sometimes outright forgeries (such as apocryphal literature) were written. We usually have condemnations of such forgeries from church authorities who were contemporaries of the writers. Also, the *Testimonium* itself is so brief that it does not match the long winded ambition of those documents which are known forgeries.

2 For example, from the time Aristotle the philosopher lived and died to the earliest copy of an Aristotle manuscript, we have a time gap of 1,400 years, yet the existence of Aristotle as a teacher and the accuracy of his writings is undisputed. (F.F. Bruce, *Archaeological Confirmation of the New Testament*).

Also, the "scholars" who reject the New Testament (and subsequent verifications) oftentimes are not historians or archaeologists but (ironically) clergymen of a liberal persuasion. One can get a Doctorate from a seminary just as he can from any other graduate school. This does not mean that we shouldn't respect such degrees or fields of study. Instead, we should be aware that subjective and specific assumptions often forge the conclusions at some (but not all) seminaries. See A.N. Sherwin-White, *Roman Law and Roman Society in the New Testament* (Baker Book House, Grand Rapids Michigan, 1994). A professor at Oxford University, he gives his appraisal of the New Testament as a historian.

3 The second century church leader Origen (185-254) states that Josephus did not believe Jesus to be the Christ (Origen, *Against Celsus* 1.47, Origen, *Commentary On Matthew Matt.* 10:17) and some take that to mean that the *Testimonium* either did not exist in his day or at least said

something different if it did exist. We should not interpret Origen's statements as evidence one way or the other, since he does not quote from, or refer directly to, the Testimonium. For reasons given earlier, Origen (just like Eusebius and others) could easily have read the *Testimonium* without concluding that Josephus was a Christian.

On the other hand, Justin Martyr gives a general reference about Jewish history affirming the resurrection of Jesus. He states confidently in his *Dialogue With Trypho* a Jew that the nation of Israel did *"learn that He (Jesus) rose from the dead,"* (*Dialogue With Trypho* CVIII, Translation from Rev. Alexander Roberts D.D. and James Donaldson LL.D editors, The Anti Nicene Fathers, Vol. 1, p. 253). He does not mention names, but this may very well have been a reference to the Josephus record.

4 Paul Barnett, ten years Master of Robert Menzies College is one who believes the *Testimonium* includes slight tampering, but that we can still reconstruct a true tradition of Josephus. He says, "Many scholars are prepared to accept much or all of the remainder of the text as genuine. I am impressed by the reference to the Christians as not being extinct "to this day" which echoes the same laissez-faire neutrality towards Christianity as shown by Josephus' fellow Pharisee Gamaliel back in the thirties (Acts 5:38-39). Also, I detect in Josephus' words "wrought surprising feats...a teacher...." an echo of yet another Pharisee, Nicodemus, who said that Jesus was a teacher who performed "signs" (John 3:2). Josephus refers to Jesus as "teacher" and "miracle worker" which supports from the comments on Nicodemus. Finally, the phrase, "a wise man" is a favorable variation of "a charlatan man" a phrase used repeatedly for the turbulent would-be miracle working prophets whom Josephus vilifies elsewhere in his writings. Since Jesus was a non-violent, non-political worker and teacher, He might well be referred to by Josephus as a "wise man." Rather than reject this abstract altogether, it seems favorable to accept it with some deletions" (Paul Barnett, *Is the New Testament Reliable?*, IVP, Downers Grove, Illinois, 1986) p. 29.

FF Bruce, (credentials listed earlier) takes a very similar position with much enthusiasm (*Jesus and Christian Origins Outside the New Testament,* pp. 32-41) as does the noted Jewish Professor Joseph Klousner, of Hebrew University (*Jesus of Nazareth*, London, 1929) pp. 55), and Dr. H. St. John Thackeray, a respected British authority on Josephus (*Josephus, The Man and The Historian*, New York, 1929, p. 125 ff). Although less committal, Dr. Bruce M. Metzger of Princeton Theological Seminary also admits to this possibility (*The New Testament, Its Background Growth and Context*, Abingdon Press, Nashville, Tennessee, 1983 pp. 73-6).

Scholars who have accepted the entire *Testimonium* as is include: F.C. Burkit, (*The Gospel History and Its Transmission*, 1906 p. 325), Michael Green, Professor of New Testament at Regents College, (*Who Is This Jesus?* Thomas Nelson Publisher, 1990 p. 117), Dr. James Kennedy, an expert on comparative religions, whose doctorate work was done at New York University (*Skeptics Answered*, Multnomah Press, 1997, p. 77) and Norman Geisler, professor of Christian Apologetics at Dallas Seminary *(Christian Apologetics*, Baker Books, 1976 p. 323). Geisler does acknowledge the possibility of the 10th century Arabic version preserved by a Syrian bishop named Agapius. William Whiston, who translated the complete works of Josephus into English also defends the entire passage . His defense can be found in an appendix at the end of the translation called Dissertation 1. Whiston was both a theologian and mathematician. A graduate of Cambridge in 1690, he succeeded Sir Isaac Newton's seat in 1703. His is the best complete English translation of Josephus.

Suggested List for Further Reading

Note: This reading list relates specifically to common apologetics topics that I do not cover thoroughly in my book. For further reading relating to my topics, see the footnotes at the end of each chapter.

Barnett, Paul, *Is the New Testament Reliable?* (IVP, Downers Grove, Illinois, 1986)

Bruce, F. F., *The New Testament Documents: Are They Reliable?* (1982)

Harrison, R. K., *Introduction to the Old Testament* (Eerdmans Publishing Company, Grant Rapids, Michigan, 1969)

Kitchen, K. A., *Ancient Orient and the Old Testament* (IVP, Downers Grove, Illinois, 1966)

Lewis, C. S., *The Problem With Pain* (Macmillan Publishing, Company, New York, N.Y., 1962)

McDowell, Josh, *Evidence That Demands a Verdict* (Here's Life Publishers Inc., San Bernardino, CA., 1979)

Metzger, Bruce M., *The New Testament, Its Background, Growth, and Content* (Abingdon Press, Nashville, Tennessee, 1983)

Ross, Hugh, *The Creator and the Cosmos* (Nav Press Publishing Group, Colorado Springs, CO., 1995)

34446345R00093

Made in the USA
San Bernardino, CA
02 May 2019